ON THE PILGRIM'S WAY

ON THE PILGRIM'S WAY

Christian Stewardship and the Tithe

John K. Brackett

MOREHOUSE PUBLISHING
Harrisburg, Pennsylvania

Copyright © 1996 John K. Brackett

MOREHOUSE PUBLISHING

Editorial Office:
871 Ethan Allen Highway
Ridgefield, CT 06877

Corporate Office:
P.O. Box 1321
Harrisburg, PA 17105

Library of Congress Cataloging-in-Publication data:
Brackett, John K.
    On the pilgrim's way : Christian stewardship and the tithe / John K. Brackett.
      p.   cm.
    ISBN: 0-8192-1663-1 (pbk.)
    1. Tithes—Biblical teaching.   2. Stewardship, Christian.
I. Title.
BV772.B65   1996
248' .6—dc20   96-23112
                                      CIP

Printed in the United States of America

CONTENTS

To Valerie and Philip

PREFACE

Stewardship is a broad topic. Stewardship can range in its focus from environmental issues to the manner in which a group of employees are best managed. The most common association with the word *stewardship*, however, is that of the fall stewardship campaign in the local congregation. From my perspective, the choice to focus on stewardship and money can be far more interesting and far more compelling when attention is turned away from the best way to go about organizing the fall campaign or the best methods to fund a parish budget. The attempt to understand the spiritual issues of Christian stewardship in the context of how to manage money and how to give money away gets to the heart of the faith issue in a person's life. Indeed, it can be an investigation into the relationship between one's life and spirituality in Christ and the way one lives out that faith in the world.

This book is designed to focus on the issue of stewardship and money. More specifically, we seek to discern the information necessary for an individual to develop a meaningful life of giving and practicing tithing as a form of Christian discipleship. The book assumes several important factors. First, it assumes that the reader is open to cultivating a life of giving away what is essential in all Christian stewardship: oneself. Without at least a willingness to consider the benefits of giving oneself to others and to God's work in the world, it is certainly not possible to develop the potential for spirituality that all of us have within ourselves.

Second, this book assumes that the reader knows practically nothing about stewardship or the practice of the tithe. Many books are available on the subject. This book seeks to bring together in a clear and careful investigation what the practice of the tithe can mean in the context of a faithful stewardship lifestyle. Our focus is upon the most important and essential principles of sound stewardship theology and practice. Many of these principles will seem strange and rather difficult at first. Nevertheless, a willingness to test these ideas in life is the most important prerequisite for a discovery of what Christian stewardship can mean for daily life in the world.

Third, this book has been written especially for people who have found their spiritual home in the Episcopal Church. However, I believe that many of the principles outlined in this book apply equally to any Christian congregation whether the parish be Roman Catholic, Orthodox, or Protestant.

In this book I advance the notion that an authentic Christian spirituality cannot develop in a person's life until a person's financial giving is at or above the standard of the tithe. Why? The reason for this will become clear in the course of the discussion. But it can be summarized here with this basic point: Almost all giving and receiving is connected in the Christian Scriptures to a person's spiritual growth in the covenant Body of Christ. For example, from the perspective of Paul, the more a person gives, the more that person becomes like the image of Christ, who gave himself for the world. As Christian stewards, we are all challenged by Paul, therefore, to become molded into the image of Christ by giving of ourselves until we discover the freedom and joy of life in covenant with Jesus Christ. This kind of giving can only be described as sacrificial. Yet, the tithe is for Paul a goal for sacrifice and a launching platform for even greater offering of one's resources. What is the reward for this sacrifice? Paul is clear about this, too. The disciple who seeks Christ through giving finds Christ!

This book is also a scholarly investigation into what the Scriptures teach about the stewardship of money. I have not tried to answer all the theological and practical questions raised in becoming a tithing steward. Rather, this book sets forth the most important principles and practices needed to begin the pilgrimage of giving.

I would like to thank several people for their help in the production of this book.

My thanks are extended to the Episcopal Church Center in New York City for a grant, which permitted me to spend time away from my regular duties as parish priest in order to write this book.

Thanks also to the Reverend Dr. Tom Carson, Laura Wright, and the Reverend Ron Reed. All three are former staff officers for the Office of Stewardship at the Episcopal Church Center in New York. To Tom, Ron, and Laura I offer my sincere appreciation and affection for all their support and help.

John K. Brackett
All Saints
1995

PART ONE

---

*The Theology of Stewardship
and the Tithe*

CHAPTER ONE

Introduction to Stewardship Theology and the Tithe

It is not uncommon for people in the Christian community today to have sincere and realistic doubts about the whole business of giving a large percentage of their income away.

This book is about Christian stewardship and the art of giving. Most people have a stereotype about the practice of stewardship. They conceive it as concerned only with money or the systematic giving away of a regular percentage of income. Many think that this whole subject is actually a gimmick for church fund raising, that talk about stewardship is nothing more than the magic words it takes to get people to cough up their money to support the church.

While it is true that the practice of Christian stewardship has something to do with church support and the way people use and allocate their finances, it certainly is not the case that stewardship is simply an attempt to manipulate people into shelling out their hard-earned money. Stewardship is not a fund-raising gimmick. It is a lifestyle, a theological philosophy of self and corporate management. For example, stewardship can serve as the management framework for the life of a Christian individual or perhaps even for an entire community. In either case, the individual or the community can discover their stewardship philosophy to be the means of empowerment for a Christian witness of their commitment in faith. This witness is made most clearly by the practice of systematically giving away a portion of time, talent, and money to accomplish some ministry in the name of Jesus Christ. The motivating force behind this generosity is simply the desire to glorify God and accomplish the work of Christ in the world.

This book is also about the practice of tithing. *Webster's New World Dictionary* defines the tithe as "one tenth of the annual produce of one's land or of one's annual income, paid as a tax or contribution to support a church or its clergy." People in the Christian community today often have sincere and realistic doubts about the whole business of giving a large percentage of their income away to some charity, particularly to the church. For most people, the idea of giving away 10 percent of their income to charity seems financially impossible and psychologically incredible. The natural question arises, why would anyone choose to give away that much money to the church or to anyone else? This book will attempt to answer that very important question.

There is also widespread controversy and confusion in the church today about the adoption of the tithe as a standard of giving. In 1982, the General Convention of the Episcopal Church affirmed the tithe as the minimum standard of giving for all Episcopalians. The Convention did not define a tithe in relation to one's annual income, perks, and tax deductions, or explain how Episcopalians should calculate it. Nevertheless, the standard of "the biblical tithe" has been affirmed by successive General Conventions in 1985, 1988 and 1991.

It has become increasingly clear since 1982 that the manner in which the tithe is understood and actually defined by modern Christians is a growing problem in different quarters of the Episcopal Church. Some say a tithe is 10 percent of one's income after taxes. Others claim that the biblical tithe is ten percent of one's gross income for the year before all taxes are paid. Still others claim that one who desires to tithe need give only what they call "the modern tithe," which is an offering of 5 percent of one's income. This study will attempt to define the actual economic nature of a tithe.

Adding to the problem of defining the tithe is the equally difficult question of where the tithe is to be given. General Convention has made no statement as to where the tithe should be offered. Many concerned Christians want to know if they should give that money only to the church? If one gives to other charities, does this count in the calculation of the tithe? These questions echo daily in the minds of people interested in Christian giving. This book will also attempt to respond to these important issues with some guidelines and to propose some ways to practice the tithe.

In our study of tithing, we shall attempt to resolve many of these problems through a careful examination of both Hebrew and Christian Scriptures. We shall also address some of the issues by means of a constructive theological discussion. However, before we can actually begin to answer some of the questions and solve some of the problems mentioned above, we must define stewardship in general. We need to understand stewardship in order to resolve some of the more difficult issues of how to practice tithing in daily life. Therefore, we must first define stewardship and its theological meaning.

What is Stewardship?

We can begin to sketch our definition by stating that stewardship is a philosophy of life and a theological form of self-management that has important implications for a person's way of living. Most Americans rarely think much about their philosophy of living. They simply live. A few folks try to live in a manner that causes them to become the happiest and best people they can be. But most people just seem to take life as it comes. This general "let it be" attitude about life, however, very often directly affects a person's happiness. Sometimes life is good and happy. But other times life's problems can shake a person to the very core. A steward thinks about life and its variable possibilities ahead of time. A steward is prepared.

Stewardship at its very foundation is a conviction that we must address on a daily basis the issue of life direction and management of self. A life of stewardship, therefore, leads a person to address his or her effectiveness and productivity in the context of daily living. In other words, stewardship must be understood as a way of life that encompasses far more than how a person uses his or her money. Stewardship is a spiritually, theologically inclusive style of life management for daily human existence.

Christian stewardship may be defined as a philosophy of management spiritually undertaken in the context of an ongoing commitment to one's covenant established in baptism with Jesus Christ. In Christian stewardship oneself and one's personal resources are used to glorify Christ and to achieve happiness, physical well-being, and spiritual growth. The central theological goal of all Christian stewardship activity is the offering of oneself for the accomplishment of Christ's work in the world. This offering of the self can be achieved through three modes: the efficient management and offering of one's time, the offering of one's talent, and the offering of one's money.

Time

Time is an important commodity. In our modern world we spend quite a bit of time trying to determine the best way to use our lives. Wasting time and making choices that cause a person to throw away their precious living time are among the most important issues of human life. The Christian steward chooses freely to organize and use his or her time for personal efficiency and greater happiness. The efficient use of time is a learned art, not something the average person instinctively knows how to do. Since the stewardship of one's time is a learned behavior, the Christian steward goes about the task of learning new management skills in their use of time. Stewards also set apart some portion of their available time for the accomplishment of Christ's work in the world.

Talent

Our talents are also an important issue in a life of Christian stewardship. Church members today seem to have many resources at their fingertips for ministry in the church. They clearly have ability, and they have the talent within themselves to achieve great things. All that they seem to lack is the faith and the courage to discover just how great they can be in the development of their talent. The Christian steward takes up the challenge of discovering his or her own talents. How does the steward do this?

The steward begins this process of self-discovery by means of reflection: an honest assessment of a person's own talents and gifts. Acting upon the process of reflection, the steward can openly seek new ways to use and develop those recognized talents in their fullness. What sets the Christian steward apart from other people who wish to expand and develop their skills and talents? The Christian steward is willing to give part of that talent to Christ's work in the world.

Money

Money is power in its purest form. Money offers anyone who has it an opportunity to achieve things that others cannot. It opens doors and makes change possible. Money comes to most of us through labor. We work, and for this work we are offered a certain amount of financial compensation. Some people use their money according to a financial plan. When a person has some kind of financial plan, they are said to *budget* their money. People who budget, spend their money with a calculated purpose or goal. Frequently, the purpose of a budget will be a simple one, such as saving dollars. Similarly, the goal of a budget may be to avoid overspending one's income or to save for the purchase of some specific item.

The way a person uses the power of their money can determine the healthy or unhealthy results of daily living. Money can help us achieve a happy life, or it can become the object of unhappiness and daily struggle. Money can even become, for some who become greedy, a reason for despair.

In modern American society most folks seem to feel that they never have enough money. This is how money can have power over any person, rich or poor. These people begin to believe that to have true happiness they must get more money. But if there is never enough money, then a person can never satisfy his or her need. Satisfaction becomes elusive and the result is a never-ending search for just a little more money. In this way people chase after money and drive themselves into despair.

The Christian steward is one who has come to grips with the power of money. He or she is willing to manage their lives and their money in such a manner that it is not necessary to seek money in order to attain happiness. Money is managed and used to bring about the happiness needed and the pursuit of money is limited because of a willingness to budget and allocate funds with purpose and care. What separates the Christian steward from others who may manage their money well for the pursuit of happiness? The Christian steward is willing to allocate some portion of his or her money to help accomplish the work of Christ in the world.

Stewardship and Spirituality

Now that we have sketched the meaning of stewardship and, more specifically, of Christian stewardship, we can consider the more mystical side of this issue. Christian stewards are committed people who are interested not only in the benefits of living by a budget and in learning how to manage their lives well. They are also spiritual people who are on a pilgrimage to God. As you probably already know, pilgrims begin their journey in one place and then travel a distance to another place in order to arrive at a holy shrine. Each pilgrim travels his or her way to that holy place for their own reasons. The travel may be hard and the journey long. Sometimes pilgrimages are filled with excitement and joy; other times the journey is slow and boring. But whatever comes is part of the process of making progress to the place of holiness. So it is for all who take up Christian stewardship as their spiritual pilgrimage. It is a pathway to a holy shrine in God. For each person it takes on its own peculiar character and meaning. So, as one goes on this pilgrimage of becoming a Christian steward, what can one expect to encounter spiritually along the way?

Grace

A person committed to Christian stewardship encounters Christ in a covenant relationship grounded in baptism. This means that the practice of stewardship is a spiritual lifestyle in which the grace of God holds a significant place. Grace can be defined as a state of being that God freely bestows on any person who responds to Christ in faith. A spiritual life grounded in stewardship addresses the issue of grace and how people use their time, talent, and money as a response to God's grace. In the spiritual life of a steward, each person offers whatever they have to Christ as a response to God. Frequently, the gift of grace generates a desire to give more and more of oneself. Over a period of time this growing desire to give from the self can develop deep spiritual meaning and roots in the self. When this growth occurs, the offering of one's money, time, and talent suddenly becomes not a task or a duty, but rather an outward and visible sign of an inward grace. In the chapters ahead we will speak more about how covenant connects to this concept of grace. Suffice it to say that grace is the mystical gift God gives to those who seek a faithful life in their covenant with Jesus Christ. And giving is a key element in how grace spiritually empowers a person's Christian growth.

A New Attitude

A lifestyle of Christian stewardship is a distinct and deeply spiritual way of living. Stewardship is also a philosophy that affects the outlook and functioning of a person. *This means fundamental change for a person's life and attitude about life.* The key to the transition into this lifestyle is, first, an ongoing examination of one's commitment to Christ, second, a desire to offer some portion of a person's time, talent, and money to Christ's work in the world, and finally, an openness to receive from God the gift of grace. How this process is lived out in a person's life varies as much as the people who commit to the stewardship lifestyle. In reality, however, one does not expect to become a Christian steward without some change to oneself or to one's former lifestyle. There is a cost to discipleship of Jesus Christ. How, specifically, does this attitude adjustment cause a person to change? The chief characteristic can be described as a growing freedom to give, which results from a willing permission to set the self in its proper place. This willingness or freedom to give ultimately leads to a change in attitude about life in general. This is truly one of the mystical characteristics of life in covenant with Jesus Christ and one of the most powerful examples of how the pilgrim is transformed by the pilgrimage. He or she becomes a new being in Christ.

Pilgrimage Leads to Community

One of the more interesting aspects of a stewardship lifestyle is that it can occur within a community of others who are striving to live the same way or among people whose lives are totally devoid of stewardship principles. Some Christian groups, even entire parishes, may practice stewardship, while others may not. Individuals can take up the philosophy of Christian stewardship and live well even though surrounded by others hostile to the idea. Stewardship is not a way of life limited to the theological customs of particular social groups or classes of people. Any Christian person or group may choose to take up the philosophy of stewardship and practice it in just about any context. In other words, almost anyone at any time can take up the stewardship lifestyle and begin the pilgrimage. The issue at stake, and the ultimate reason for taking the pilgrim's way, however, is usually the same. Each person or group takes up a life of stewardship in order to begin a pilgrimage of giving, the goal being a deeper sense of glorifying God and a deeper spirituality and personal investment in Christ's saving covenant.

This decision to become a pilgrim has a mystical result. Those who begin this pilgrimage may share nothing in common. But they all end their pilgrimages at the same holy shrine: Jesus Christ and service to him in the world. Paradoxically, those who had nothing in common now share in a mystical vision in which Christ is their unity, though each still maintains his or her individual uniqueness.

This is truly a mystical and spiritual miracle ignored by many: that all who take up a pilgrimage toward Christ end their journeys as sons and daughters of God.

Salvation and the Pilgrim's Way

Now we come to the deepest and most important aspect of the stewardship pilgrimage: the relationship between salvation and stewardship. One who takes up the pilgrimage ultimately discovers Jesus Christ at the center of their lives. But how this happens is so mystical and particular to the individual that it cannot be discussed as being this or that way. It is a reality as special for each person as their own individuality.

It may seem strange to relate Christian stewardship to the richness of salvation, but the two are indeed integrally associated. The philosophy of stewardship, like all other aspects of Christianity, is deeply linked to a person's spirituality and authenticity in the faith. If a person's spirituality and faith is strong and energetic, he or she can be zealous in personal management and in personal stewardship of God's gifts. If a person's faith is riddled with ambivalence, then that person is motivated only to be average and perhaps may even fall below the spiritual standards they may say they want to follow in their lives.

Salvation is a complicated word to define but briefly and simply put, for the Christian, it means to be in a covenant with Jesus Christ and to grow in faith through discipleship. Salvation also means that a person wishes to be molded into Christ's image by being freed from sin and death in this world and promised new life in the next. For the modern Christian, the biblical image of covenant and of following Jesus has many meanings. Often it is terribly difficult to grasp. In this study, we shall attempt to grasp what it means to live in covenant with Jesus Christ. For what cannot be grasped intellectually is even more difficult to live out in daily life. This is especially the case today for anyone whose "heart is set on the pilgrim's way," who wishes to make a personal pilgrimage of discipleship to follow Jesus. How does one go about discovering how these two factors of living out a life of stewardship and one's salvation actually relate to each other? A person who begins the pilgrimage of giving by actively taking up the philosophy of Christian stewardship will begin to find an answer to this question by considering the following.

First, the Christian faith can only truly begin to take hold in a person's life in a serious and evident manner when that person is willing to receive the gift of salvation. God has given us salvation through the life and sacrifice of Jesus Christ. This means that God has begun the process of our salvation by offering us a gift, the gift of grace. In order to receive this gift of God, a person must be open to the notion of "receiving." Obviously, one who would truly be a Christian disciple must be willing to receive divine things from God in order to enter a new realm of spirituality. Once these divine things are accepted and internally integrated, a person usually makes progress in discipleship. Disciples begin their work by receiving more and more from their teacher. So it is with the Christian steward. By receiving the gift of God's grace, the disciple begins the salvation process in earnest.

A pilgrimage of stewardship begins, therefore, in relation to Jesus Christ, and personal salvation begins with the practice of receiving God's gift. From receiving this gift, the steward can begin to grasp that Christian worship is a response to God's gift. One worships God and makes offerings in thanksgiving for the benefits of salvation. The practice of giving is linked spiritually to Christian worship in this manner. To give away some part of oneself in the name of one's faith in Jesus Christ gets at the motivation behind the practice of systematic giving as a way of worshiping God. Since a stewardship lifestyle in which a person practices systematic and regular giving helps a person learn both how to give and how to receive, a life of stewardship practice is fundamental and perhaps even essential for meaning and for appreciation of Christian worship. Christians who take up the pilgrimage of being a steward inevitably become more interested and more attached to a worshiping community because they see and understand that this is the social context in which they can best express their desire to offer back to God spiritually some part of themselves.

Second, Christian faith develops in people who live in the world and relate to the world's economy. For the steward, living in the world's economy includes giving and receiving as an integrated form of spiritual and physical lifestyle. If someone wants to receive grace, he or she must be prepared to look honestly at their own lives and consider ways to improve the management of themselves. Does their lifestyle exhibit good management? Does their lifestyle demonstrate an ability to give part of themselves away? These important questions require careful consideration.

The Christian steward must also evaluate how he or she acts in the work place. What kind of a manager or worker is he or she? How well does one use time and talents in the world? Is one's work truly productive? Is there a better way to do one's job? The point here is simple. An attitude about work comes with a life of Christian stewardship. The attitude is not one of defensiveness with regard to learning. Rather, Christian stewards can work in the real world and learn to make themselves better by being willing to hear others who make good suggestions or others who know better ways. The Christian steward is not afraid to learn new ways. The Christian steward is willing to learn without clinging proudly to the tried and true ways of the past. Thus, one more mystical benefit of the stewardship pilgrimage is a new attitude in the work place, an attitude that can lead to greater economic success and happiness.

Stewards and the Covenant

The Bible is the central source of inspiration for Christians. Many passages in the Bible tell the story of the interaction between God and humankind as a story of covenant, a relationship based upon promise. Someone who decides to take up the discipleship of Jesus in the manner of a Christian steward *reaffirms such a relationship with God.* By reaffirming one's commitment to Christ made at baptism, promises are made and expectations are reaffirmed as well. Modern Christians have lost a general appreciation for the fact that the Christian faith has historically portrayed itself as a way of life in a covenant with Jesus Christ. When Jesus, for example, celebrates the Lord's Supper with his disciples, he makes a covenant with them. The covenant is the promise that, every time they drink the wine or eat the bread in memory of Jesus, they do so remembering the promises of the kingdom of God and of Jesus himself, until the kingdom comes into fulfillment. This Lord's Supper covenant is between God and those who hold dear the promises of Jesus, and it relates directly to promises made about God's kingdom and the coming reign of God on earth. But how many Christians realize clearly, when they go forward to receive communion, that they are by their participation in the service actually proclaiming to themselves and to the world that they want God to reign in themselves and in the world and that they hold dear the promises of Jesus concerning this coming reign of God? Many Christians fail to realize the full import of this heavenly banquet and its significance. Why? Because they have not yet connected with this special service the reaffirmation of their faith in the covenant made with Jesus Christ at baptism.

In our subsequent chapters, we shall see in a deeper sense the actual roots and elements of Christian covenant. For the moment, however, we can state that in general the covenant Christ makes with each Christian disciple at baptism is indissoluble. But for the disciple to experience the covenant in all its fullness, he or she must reaffirm in two important ways the vows and promises made therein. A disciple of Jesus must be prepared to reaffirm his or her faith in God, and a disciple must be willing to receive spiritual gifts from God following their reaffirmation of the covenant. The result is a more keen appreciation of the mystical meaning of life in the covenant with Jesus Christ.

Stewardship and Ownership

Another mystical characteristic comes to the pilgrim of stewardship. Someone committed to life as a Christian steward ultimately develops a new attitude toward ownership and Creation. The steward begins to understand that Creation is owned ultimately by the Creator, not by the created. In other words, the steward develops a theology of Creation in which God comes to be understood as the ultimate owner of all things. For people active in the world, this means that one's role in Creation is to manage, not to exploit. There is a genuine difference between a person who approaches Creation as a steward and another person who does not. What is this difference? Albert Schweitzer writes clearly of it in his magnificent autobiography, *Out of My Life and Thought.*[1] In this theological and personal masterpiece, Schweitzer advocates an attitude he calls "a reverence for life." Reverence for life is simply the attitude that Creation is valuable in itself. Therefore, Creation is due respect and gentle care. A Christian steward develops this same attitude toward others and towards life on this planet. The Christian steward views Creation as a product of a sacred process. It is, therefore, worthy of ethical management, not exploitation.

For Schweitzer, reverence for life is a person's commitment to life as precious and important in and of itself. Similarly, the Christian steward views life and Creation as precious. We come into this world, stay only a short while, and then die. So we must not use recklessly those things that are here for us to use as we arrive and that stay on Planet Earth long after we depart by death. To be sure, it is possible to handle Creation with some freedom. However, human industrial history has shown quite conclusively that human license has led to the abuse of Creation.

Entering the Christian covenant of Jesus Christ in a lifestyle of stewardship means that a person is forced to assess his or her attitudes toward Creation and life on this earth. Through this process, the steward receives the gifts of wonder, appreciation, and reverence for all Creation.

Reflection

The final mystical characteristic of a pilgrim on the pilgrim's way of the steward is honest and healthy self-reflection. For becoming a Christian steward initiates an inner journey of ever growing personal assessment. For most people, reflection is a difficult and slippery experience because reflection forces us to examine ourselves thoroughly and to assess hidden strengths and weaknesses in an honest way. The process of reflection is the practice of looking inward with justice and acceptance. It is a willingness to examine our assets and our liabilities.

In order for someone to understand completely what stewardship means, they must be willing to come under judgment and assess their ethical and moral standards with genuine rigor and justice. Is one's lifestyle manageable and equitable for others as well as for oneself? Do one's daily actions reflect reverence for life? Are one's judgments ethical and moral for all concerned? The answers to these questions become clear only through an authentic willingness to reflect honestly on oneself and to have others offer an assessment as well. For most, this kind of personal assessment is an ego-deflating experience. Nevertheless, it is necessary in order to learn and to grow. Through the grace of God, the Christian steward can receive the gift of courage and the ego-strength required for such an honest reflective process.

With the aid of reflection, a Christian steward can recognize spiritually the central foundation of his or her commitment in life. Am I committed to the world, its money, power, and prestige? Or am I committed to the divine economy, which beckons each of us to manage well and to give ourselves to God's work on earth? For the Christian steward, reflection leads to a decision about what is important in life: God or things.

Conclusion

Now that we have surveyed some of the results of life along the pilgrim's way of being a steward, it should be clear that stewardship is far more than a gimmick to get people to give money to the church. It is, in fact, a complete misunderstanding of stewardship to think that it is just designed to trick people for fund-raising purposes. As we have seen, stewardship is, rather, a way of life that involves a covenant with God. Stewardship also involves the development of all that a person can be. It is a management lifestyle that emphasizes a willingness to give and receive. And finally, stewardship involves the commitment and the offering of a portion of our time, talent, and money for God's work in the world. But how much is a portion?

We shall now turn to the Hebrew Scriptures in order to understand the biblical portions of the tithe. In the next chapter we shall also begin the process of answering some of the difficult questions we have raised concerning the tithe. We do this ever seeking to demonstrate the biblical basis of stewardship and the joy of being free to give.

CHAPTER TWO

Stewardship Theology, the Hebrew Scriptures, and the Tithe

The Hebrew concept of the tithe is integrally linked to Hebrew thinking about the covenant.

We now turn our attention to an investigation of the tithe in the Hebrew Scriptures. The tithe is a standard of giving set forth in a long and complicated series of Hebrew traditions. This history of tithe theology and practice can be traced, but there are numerous problems. One of the problems is that critical historical research of the Old Testament in the last one hundred years has demonstrated that the various traditions in the Pentateuch, and some of the other books in the Hebrew canon, have their origin in several writers and editors in different periods of Hebrew history.[1] Our study cannot begin to investigate all the results of this research and its ramifications for an understanding of Judaism. However, some of the findings can help us interpret the most important passages concerned with tithing. Our study of the tithe starts with Genesis.

Genesis

Sacrifice was a significant and highly important topic among the Hebrews. It was commonly understood in ancient Israel as the sacrifice of animals on an altar to Yahweh. In the tradition found in Gen. 8:20-22, we are told by the Yahwist writer that sacrifice on an altar commemorates a covenant and an intentional thankfulness to Yahweh:

> *Noah built an altar for Yahweh, and choosing*
> *from all the clean animals and all the*
> *clean birds he offered burnt offerings*
> *on the altar. Yahweh smelt the appeasing fragrance*

> *and said to himself, "Never again will I curse*
> *the earth because of Man."*[2]

In this passage, following the establishment of Yahweh's new covenant with Noah, the writer describes how Noah built an altar in thanksgiving and sacrificed burnt offerings to Yahweh. We are also told that Yahweh was pleased by the offerings. It is important to note, therefore, that the sacrifice of animals begins in Genesis as a response to Yahweh's generosity and graciousness through the covenant relationship. Noah has believed the promises of Yahweh. He has stayed the course and come through the great Flood with his life and his family, just as Yahweh has promised. Hence, Noah is thankful and ready to make a sacrifice in response to God's faithful keeping of the promises made in the covenant with him and his family.

We see the same kind of structure and story in the case of the covenant established with Abram, described in Genesis12:1-12. There we find a similar association of altar sacrifice with thankfulness to Yahweh.

> *Yahweh said to Abram, "Leave your country,*
> *your family and your father's house, for the*
> *land I will show you. I will make you a great*
> *nation; I will bless you and make your name*
> *so famous that it will be used as a blessing."*

When Yahweh calls Abram and establishes a covenant with him, Yahweh offers Abram a choice. Yahweh promises that if Abram will go to a foreign land, he will be blessed. The choice that Abram must make is simple. Does Abram believe Yahweh and go to the land he will be shown, or does Abram play it safe and stay where he is? Yahweh does not threaten or force Abram to make the choice. It is simply placed before Abram. Abram chooses to accept the promise of Yahweh and to go. Upon arrival, Abram responds to Yahweh in thanksgiving by offering an animal sacrifice on an altar. Yahweh promises Abram that his ancestors shall be numerous and that his children shall inhabit the Promised Land.

A new dimension, however, is added to the notion of covenant in the Abram tradition. It is the personal decision of Abram to give away a portion of his personal assets as an act of faithfulness. The story is told in Genesis 14:17-20. There we read of Abram's response to God's high priest, Melchizedek.

> *When Abram came back after the defeat of*
> *Chedor-laomer and the kings who had been*
> *on his side, the king of Sodom came to meet*
> *him in the Valley of Shaveh (that is, the Valley*
> *of the King). Melchizedek, king of Salem*
> *brought bread and wine; he was a priest*
> *of God Most High. He pronounced this blessing,*
> *"Blessed be Abram by God Most High, creator of*
> *heaven and earth, and blessed be*
> *God Most High for handing over your*
> *enemies to you." And Abram gave him a*
> *tithe of everything.*

Abram presents a proportion of all his worldly goods to Melchizedek. The offering of the tithe is presented in response to a blessing offered by the priest of God Most High (*EL Elyon*). We are told that Abram offers 10 percent of his worldly goods to Melchizedek in thanksgiving for God's blessing and for Abram's deliverance from his enemies.

This is the first reference to the tithe in Genesis. The practice of percentage giving developed early in the structure of Genesis as an example of and the model for a personal offering to God. Obviously, this offering is a way of showing appreciation for blessings. The offering is apparently directed in this case specifically for the use of the priest, Melchizedek. Perhaps the writer of this passage is attempting to justify tithes as a form of support for the priesthood.

Whether the passage is such an attempt or not, it nevertheless offers the critical investigator some insight into the early understanding of covenant. At this level of the tradition, the tithe is an outward sign of faithfulness to the covenant. The tithe completes the concrete exchange between God and humanity. God has offered a relationship based upon promise, and in response a human makes a concrete sacrifice in two forms: whole burnt offerings on an altar and a personal tithe of all worldly goods. Hence, the tithe, at this point in the tradition, is considered a witness of faithfulness in response to God.

Exodus

In Exodus, where the early traditions of the Passover are outlined, we can trace another expression of the definition of offering and its connection to covenant. Passages beginning in Exodus 12 show that sacrifice and certain cultic offerings are suggested in relation to the Passover covenant. Unlike Genesis, however, the directions for these offerings are quite distinct, elaborate, and complicated. We cannot investigate all of these types of offerings, but one text in particular is important. It concerns the offering of the first fruits.

In Exod. 22:29, one of the cultic offering directives orders that "the first fruits" and the first born both of all in Israel and of all animals in Israel, be dedicated to Yahweh. The reason for this dedication is related to the Hebrew covenant and is spelled out in Exodus 13. Yahweh claims Israel, promises to fulfill the covenant by delivering the Hebrews from the Egyptians, and expects them to journey to the Promised Land. In response to these benefits, Israel must dedicate the first fruits of all her labor and life to Yahweh in thankfulness.

These passages of Exodus make clear that the dedication of the first born and the first fruits has nothing to do with the concept of the tithe. The two are separate and unrelated offerings to Yahweh. In fact, the tithe is not mentioned in Exodus in relation to the Passover. The offerings in these passages apparently are understood as the literal first issue of all yields in Israel. Percentages of these yields are not mentioned.

Leviticus

In Lev. 27:30-31, we have a later tradition that clearly demands the offering of the tithe. However, Leviticus offers no clear directions about the practice of tithing, what a tithe is and how it is to be administered. The passage in question simply reads as follows:

> *All tithes of the land, levied on the produce*
> *of the earth or the fruits of trees, belong to*
> *Yahweh; they are consecrated to Yahweh. If*
> *a man wishes to redeem part of his tithe, he*
> *must add one-fifth to its value.*

Note that neither the priest nor the sanctuary are mentioned. More than likely, however, both are understood as the logical recipients of that which is "consecrated to Yahweh." The instructions are vague, with the exception of directions for those who wish to redeem their tithe. Those persons who wish to redeem must add one fifth more to the amount. No connection is made to the Passover concept of the first fruits.

Deuteronomy

In the later traditions of Deut. 14:22-29, we find more specific information regarding the offering of the tithe. The Deuteronomist writer directs that there be two types of regular tithing. First, the Israelite is to offer an *annual tithe*. The writer specifies how the annual tithe is to be collected and spent. These directions are different from what the modern reader might expect. The directions specify that this tithe is to be spent on oneself!

> *Every year you must take a tithe of all that*
> *your sowing yields on the land, and in the*
> *presence of Yahweh your God, in the place*
> *that he chooses to give his name a home, you*
> *are to eat the tithe of your corn, your wine*
> *and your oil and the first-born of your herd*
> *and flock; so shall you learn to fear Yahweh*
> *your God always.*

These directions require the person who tithes to go to a place and to eat the tithe there. Apparently, the annual tithe is not turned over to either the sanctuary or the priesthood but is actually used for cultic celebration in the name of Yahweh. The writer also connects this to the concept of the first fruits. For the writer of this section of Deuteronomy, the annual tithe is definitely connected to the Passover covenant. Its yield is in keeping with the doctrine of the first fruits of Israel belonging to Yahweh. Hence, the text implies that the offering is comprised of the first born of all animals and the tithe of the yield of the crops.

We read further in this passage:

> *If the road is too long for you, if you cannot*
> *bring your tithe because the place in which*
> *Yahweh chooses to make a home for his*

> *name is too far, when Yahweh your God has*
> *blessed you, you must turn your tithe into*
> *money, and with the money clasped in your*
> *hand you must go to the place chosen by Yahweh;*
> *there you may spend the money on*
> *whatever you like, oxen, sheep, wine, strong*
> *drink, anything your heart desires. You are to*
> *eat there in the presence of Yahweh your*
> *God and rejoice, you and your household. Do*
> *not neglect the Levite who lives in your*
> *towns, since he has no share or inheritance*
> *with you.*

The second kind of tithe is that of the *triennial tithe*. The tithe set aside every third year is designated for the use of the needy, in particular the Levite clergy, strangers in the land, orphans, and widows. The third year tithe is, therefore, directly connected to Jewish hospitality laws. These laws require the Israelites to provide for strangers and for the needs of orphans, widows, and the poor in their local community. The Deuteronomist in this section also connects this tithe to provision for the clergy. It enables the Levitical clergy to count on being supported by the people. It appears, however, at least in Deuteronomy, that the clergy are not provided for on a regular annual basis.

Thus, the Deuteronomist writer of these sections of Deuteronomy recognizes two kinds of tithe. Both types are understood as important expressions of personal offering and of faith. Both kinds of tithe are apparently set in the context of and linked to the first fruits concept of the Passover. By offering the annual tithe in celebration of Yahweh before the seat of Yahweh, the Israelite expresses joy and faith in Yahweh and Yahweh's covenant. By offering the third year tithe to the needy and to the clergy, the faithful Israelite lives up to the communal laws of Yahweh and Yahweh's demand for hospitality to the poor as set forth in the Law.

Nehemiah

By the time of the Second Temple and the late traditions associated with the Book of Nehemiah, we find that the various traditions of offering tithes and first fruits have become fully integrated and joined with the additional needs of clergy and the Temple. In

Nehemiah, there is no longer any question about the nature or the practice of tithing. Neh. 10:21-39, for example, demonstrates clearly that the tithes of the people and the first fruits of the land are joined to a temple obligation. The tone of the text is that of a required tax on the people.[3]

> *We recognize the following obligations: to*
> *give one third of a shekel yearly for the liturgical*
> *requirements of the Temple of our God;*
> *for the loaves set out, for the perpetual oblation,*
> *for the perpetual holocaust, for the*
> *sacrifices on Sabbaths, on New moon feasts*
> *and on solemnities, for sacred foods, for*
> *sacrifices for sin to atone for Israel; in short,*
> *for all the services of the Temple of our God;*
> *and further, to bring yearly to the Temple of*
> *of our God the first-fruits of our soil and the*
> *first-fruits of every fruit of every tree, also the*
> *firstborn of our sons and of our cattle, as it is*
> *written in the Law—those first-born of our*
> *herds and flocks taken to the Temple of our*
> *God being intended for the priests officiating*
> *in the Temple of our God. Furthermore, we*
> *will bring to the priest, to the chambers*
> *of the Temple of our God, the best of our meal,*
> *the fruit of every tree, new wine and oil; and*
> *to the Levites the tithe on our soil—the*
> *Levites themselves will collect the tithes*
> *from all our agricultural towns.*

By the time of the Second Temple, the tithe has become attached to an actual religious tax on the people of Israel. The people are under obligation to pay these taxes to the Levitical clergy at appointed times.

For Nehemiah, the clergy are expected to place the tithes, offerings, and taxes in the treasury of the Temple. The clergy are expected to administer these and to set aside a tenth of the tithe taxes for the daily operation of the Temple.

What Is the Tithe?

In a most brief and rudimentary way, we have seen that the

Hebrew concept of the tithe is integrally linked to Hebrew thinking about the covenant. We have also seen that the tithe is an embodiment of Hebrew sacrifice and offering. The tithe is closely associated with the concept of covenant faithfulness. In addition, we have demonstrated that the practice and meaning of the tithe is at many points in the Hebrew tradition vague and outright difficult to understand. Nevertheless, we can summarize what most of the traditions in the Hebrew Scriptures do seem to accept as a concept of the tithe. Let us begin with the material that is consistent and universally supported in the Hebrew traditions.

Tithe offerings are recorded in early Hebrew writings as an extension of a covenant relationship in which animal sacrifice holds a central position. As time progresses, the tithe develops as a separate, personal financial offering, and it becomes an actual formal practice of the Hebrew covenant relationship with Yahweh. The practice of tithing eventually evolves in the Hebrew tradition toward theological connection with the financial support of the Temple and the clergy. In the course of this evolutionary process, the relationship of the tithe to the clergy and to the theology of the Passover constantly changes. However, during these various fluctuations, it appears that the practice of the tithe is understood to contain certain commonly accepted conditions.

Conditions for the Tithe

The practice of tithing is an outward sign of an Israelite's acceptance of Yahweh's authority in the covenant partnership. A tithe is not offered to Yahweh because the person simply feels like giving something back to Yahweh. Rather, the act of giving to Yahweh the produce (or the money) resulting from agricultural activity is understood to be a simple and joyful acknowledgment of the covenant relationship. It is an outward response in practice to a serious contractual covenant in which pledges and promises are made and honored regularly. The faithfulness of Israel is expressed in the tithe and its joyful blessings. Some Hebrew writings stress that Israel offers a tithe because Yahweh is due a certain percentage of all economic activity.

Hebrew writers constantly make it clear that an offering of Israel's yield demonstrates that Israel belongs to Yahweh in covenant. The tithe offering is, therefore, set in the context of a joyful recognition that Yahweh's authority extends over Israel. In return for this authority, however, Yahweh offers Israel many blessings and the joy of salvation manifested in divine grace. Thus, the tithe is a concrete expression of acceptance of Yahweh's authority. It also recalls the blessings of Yahweh and the community's faith. Through the practice of the tithe, Israel confirms its belief in the authority of Yahweh and Yahweh's promises. Ultimately, Yahweh will fulfill all of the covenant promises and complete the salvation of Israel.

The concept of the first born and first fruits dedication, which originated in connection with the Passover tradition and probably was a separate practice from the tithe, eventually becomes associated with the practice of tithing. In later traditions, the tithe and the concept of the first fruits are closely associated. This is especially true of traditions influenced by the Deuteronomist and the Temple. Thus, in late Jewish traditions, the tithe became linked to an offering of the first fruits of all labor and success to Yahweh as a response of thankfulness to the blessing of participation in the Hebrew covenant.

While the tithe is not always practiced in the same way for all traditions within Judaism, it is, nevertheless, found in all but the Exodus tradition. Thus, the tithe is, practically speaking, a universally accepted form of offering worship and thanksgiving toward Yahweh, and it marks the Israelite as specifically and faithfully devoted to the covenant.

Problems and Issues

We have seen some conflicts in the manner in which the tithe is presented and practiced. In some cases, references authorizing the practice of tithing appear vague about how the tithe is to be calculated and distributed.

In most Hebrew texts, tithing is taught outright, or it is assumed that the tithe is practiced on an annual basis. The triennial tithe adds somewhat to the confusion. In most cases, the amount appears to be based upon the gross yearly income—the "produce." The role of the first fruits and the first born—are they part of or additions to the tithe?—adds to the lack of clarity.

Tithe to Whom?

Another problem is the issue of who is to receive the tithe. On this issue, conflicts arise between the various writers and their traditions. The number and types of recipients vary and can be listed as follows:

> The tithe is sometimes understood as a direct gift to the clergy for their continued maintenance.

> The tithe is sometimes understood as an annual offering of joy to be used by the people to celebrate the name of Yahweh and covenant relationship. The people consume this tithe themselves in the context of a cultic celebration.

> Certain collections of the tithe in the third year are understood as designated for the use of the poor, the sojourner, the needy, and the Levitical clergy.

Hebrew Theologies of Giving

Now that we have surveyed the traditions and practices of tithing in the Hebrew Scriptures, we can summarize also the basic theological thinking behind these traditions.

A Theology of Obligation

As we have seen in our survey of the Hebrew traditions concerning the tithe, at times certain Hebrew writers make a theological appeal to the legal obligation of the people to support their Temple and their clergy because Yahweh has commanded it. The theology behind this kind of approach is that of covenant obligation. Israel is in a contract with Yahweh. The writers exhort Israel to keep the terms of the contract by paying its tithe regularly. This theology generally interprets the tithe in connection with the first fruits and first born mentioned in Exodus. What the faithful community feels about this obligation to offer the tithe is either unimportant or deemphasized. For those who take this theological view seriously, the main point is to affirm that God's work is done through the Temple, and this sacred work must be supported by the tithes of the people. In this theological tradition, those who keep their obligation of tithing to the Temple are understood to be practicing their faith and keeping the covenant. Since they pay their tithes, these people are, for all intents and purposes, viewed as good and faithful Jews.

A Theology of Devotion

Other Hebrew writers present theological viewpoints in support of tithing by showing how the people make their offerings of the tithe in faith and from the heart. The people are portrayed as doing this because they love Yahweh and wish to demonstrate their devotion to their God. They see their gifts, not as obligations, but as precious expressions of their covenant faith. God's work in this tradition is understood as that of blessing the people and of providing for the needs of those who are less fortunate. The offering of a tithe is viewed as an act that honors Yahweh. It demonstrates openly an expression of corporate devotion. Emphasis is placed on the community's feeling instead of on the legal requirements.

A Theology of Gratitude

Finally, there is the theological tradition of offerings made to the clergy and the Temple as freewill faith offerings to Yahweh. These gifts are offered in thanksgiving for all that Yahweh has done for Israel. They are a response from the heart of Israel to Yahweh's cult, and they celebrate Yahweh's greatness. Israel is grateful, seeing that Yahweh demonstrates love for Israel by blessing her with many good things. In effect, these offerings are grounded in a theology of gratitude for Yahweh and Yahweh's many blessings.

Voluntary Contributions

Another tradition of giving in the Hebrew Scriptures has nothing to do with the practice of the tithe, but it is certainly relevant to the discussion of it. This tradition concerns the building of a sacred place for Yahweh and voluntary giving. Voluntary giving can best be discussed in the context of two specific references from the Hebrew Scriptures.

Exodus 25

In Exodus 25, voluntary giving is described and set forth by the Hebrew writer as a fundamental way to support the sanctuary of Yahweh. "Yahweh spoke to Moses and said, 'Tell the sons of Israel to set aside a contribution for me; you shall accept this contribution from every man whose heart prompts him to give it'" (Exod. 25:1-2). Contributions to the sanctuary are considered a regular and significant part of personal faith and sacrifice to Yahweh. Note that these contributions are not mentioned in connection with the tithe. They are voluntary offerings for the building of the sacred place, in addition to regular annual gifts.

1 Chronicles 29

In 1 Chronicles 29, a further development in the understanding of voluntary offering is set forth. King David announces that he has voluntarily donated a large portion of his wealth toward the building of the palace Temple. David is then quoted as making this announcement:

> With all the resources I have, I have
> provided for the house of my God, adding
> gold to gold, silver to silver, bronze to bronze,
> iron to iron, wood to wood, onyx, inlaid
> stones, colored and striped stones, precious
> stones of every kind, masses of alabaster.
> What is more; what gold and silver I have in
> my own treasury I give out of love for the
> house of my God, over and above what I
> have provided already for the holy Temple—
> three thousand talents of gold, gold of Ophir,
> seven thousand talents of refined silver for
> plating the walls of the building. Whatever
> gold you have, whatever silver, or workmanship
> of the craftsman's hand, which of you
> today will undertake to consecrate it to Yahweh?

The result of this call for a voluntary offering is an overwhelming response. All of David's monetary gifts to the Temple are exceeded by gifts of the leaders of Israel and the people. In 1 Chron. 29:9-10, we are also told of the reaction of the people and of David to this outpouring of great generosity toward Yahweh.

> The people rejoiced at what these had given so readily, since
> their generous gift to Yahweh had been made wholeheartedly.
> King David too was filled with joy. In the sight of the whole
> assembly David blessed Yahweh.

At this, the Chronicle writer records that David sang a song. It is a song of praise to Yahweh. David sings as a representative of the people, and he offers thanks to Yahweh for generosity in Israel:

> *Yahweh our God, this store we have*
> *provided to build a house for your holy name,*
> *all comes from your hand, all is yours. O my*
> *God, you search the heart, I know, and*
> *delight in honesty, and with honesty of heart*
> *I have willingly given all this; and now with*
> *joy I have seen your people here offer you*
> *their gifts willingly. Yahweh, God of our ancestors,*
> *of Abraham, of Isaac, of Israel, watch*
> *over this for ever, shape the purpose of your*
> *people's heart and direct their hearts to you.*

We see in 1 Chronicles the example of a voluntary offering motivated by faith from the heart. We see that as a extension of sacrifice, the offering has attained another meaning as it is associated with a personal faith and obedience to the covenant. These offerings are a voluntary gift from the people for the building of Yahweh's Temple and for the Temple's regular upkeep. Like the traditions found in Exodus 25, the offering of one's money to the work of building the sacred place for Yahweh does not take the place of the regular tithe sacrifices. Rather, the voluntary offering is a sign of Israel's faithfulness to Yahweh.

Thus, voluntary giving is the spontaneous outpouring of faithfulness and love from one who acts as a full partner in the covenant. The writer of Chronicles exalts this form of making an offering because it reveals the ultimate willingness of Israel to sacrifice and be shaped in history and in personhood by Yahweh's divine will.

Christian Theology and Hebrew Traditions of Giving

Our survey of the Hebrew Scriptures and the Hebrew theology of stewardship has shown that a tradition of both tithing and voluntary giving existed in Israel. This tradition was based upon the notion of a personal sacrificial offering and responsible thankfulness for the blessing of Yahweh through the covenant. We have also seen, however, that by no means do the writers of the Hebrew Scriptures agree about the actual practice of tithing and what it means theologically.

We can now deal with some of the issues that we raised in the first chapter. In particular, we can address the issue of the calculation of a tithe. Our study of the Hebrew Scriptures has made it abundantly clear why this is such an issue for Christians interested in tithing. The tithing tradition in the Hebrew Scriptures does not provide a consistent guide for calculating a tithe.

We have also seen that the Hebrew Scriptures reveal another problem for Christians. The traditions concerning the tithe maintain no unity concerning what a tithe actually is. The earlier the tradition, the more vague the text. The later the text, the more clear and defined these issues appear to be. Still, none of the traditions ever set down an absolute rule or method to resolve these problems.

Since the Hebrew Scriptures are composed of many different traditions, from many different time periods, it should come as no surprise to the investigator that wide variations of interpretation and practice existed. As time passed, editors of the various traditions and teachings about the tithe made every effort to resolve some of the problems by streamlining their views or by attempting to reconcile earlier statements and theologies. In some cases, however, the editors of the traditions were never able to reconcile certain questions and issues of practice and procedure.

Unfortunately, many modern Christian writers on the topic of tithing have ignored these facts. Christian authors have instead tended to advance the Hebrew references to tithing as absolute authority for tithing practices among Christians. In many cases, they have advanced arguments for the practice of tithing based upon a selection of Hebrew verses that accommodates a simple authoritarian viewpoint. Indeed, these viewpoints can be summarized in four main points.

> 1. The tithe is an obligation set down by Scripture and is required of all Christians. Christians ought, therefore, to meet their obligation set out in Scripture and confirm that the Scriptures are true by tithing.

> 2. The tithe ought to be defined as the first fruits of all one's income for a year. Christians should, therefore, offer their first fruits to the church by tithing on their gross incomes.

Any other gifts to charity are voluntary and should be made only after gifts to the church.

3. A tithe is a Jewish practice, but it is also Christian because Jesus does not denounce the tithe, nor does Jesus deny that the tithe is a good standard of giving.

4. Christians who tithe fulfill their Christian obligation to the church and to God's covenant through Jesus Christ.

In response to Christian authors who use Hebrew Scripture to advance these arguments for the practice of tithing, our study has demonstrated the following principles.

First, the practice of tithing is integrally associated in the Hebrew Scriptures with personal and corporate worship and related more specifically to the practice of sacrifice. Generally, this fact has been ignored by the majority of Christian authors who write about the tithe. Christian authors have tended rather to argue in favor of tithing from the point of view of the importance of Old Testament scriptural authority. While one certainly would not deny scriptural authority, the argument that one should practice tithing in order to preserve the authority of Scripture is unconvincing. This kind of argument appears to contend that the authority of Scripture cannot stand on its own without human faithfulness through tithing. Christians need not practice the tithe in order to save Scripture's authority, but certainly Christians ought to consider what implications the practice of tithing holds for a spiritual life of sacrificial faith in God.

Second, the theology and practice of tithing is integrally connected in the Hebrew Scriptures to Yahweh's various covenants with Israel. The kinds of arguments offered by Christian authors in favor of tithing, usually by citing the Hebrew Scriptures for authority, practically never mention even the basic definitions of covenant relationship. Hence, since the tithe is taken out of its proper context of the covenant with Yahweh, the arguments in favor of tithing must be out of context as well. Unfortunately, the Christian appeal for tithing, without the setting of the covenant, can only be interpreted by open-minded Christians as an attempt to use the Hebrew Scripture for the purpose of fund raising and not a serious appeal to the deeper spiritual meaning of offering and sacrifice in a covenant with God. As we have seen, Christians ought to consider the tithe as a viable form of giving because they wish to share the covenant partnership with God in a more serious and tangible form.

Third, while some Christians today do, in fact, view their faith in Christ as containing a covenant relationship, they also appear to have the common misconception that, like the Jewish dietary laws of the Old Testament, the tithe has been superseded by the New Covenant of Christ. In other words, they believe that the tithe is a Jewish practice and that it has nothing to do with the Christian faith. Our investigation of the Hebrew Scripture has called this viewpoint into question. Clearly, the covenant is the appropriate setting for the practice of tithing. Since this is the case, the Christian covenant with Christ needs to be examined as to whether it, too, is the proper setting for a similar practice of the tithe.

In subsequent chapters we will examine the compatibility of the tithe concept with the Christian covenant as found in the Christian Scriptures. But for now we can at the minimum point out the following. Christians need to be open to the possibility that the Church is challenging them to tithe because the Church hopes for them to enter the pilgrims' journey as members of a covenant with God. They must also understand that the spiritual aspects of covenant are supported by the authority of both the Old and the New Testaments. Hence, all practices associated with covenant are theologically sound and important for the full benefits of salvation.

Fourth, as our study has clearly shown, the linkage of the first fruits is a late addition to the tithe tradition. To make the first fruits doctrine into the key determining factor in the calculation of a tithe is simply to manipulate the tradition. Christians who choose to offer the first fruits of all their labors might contribute their first paycheck annually, or a contribution "off the top." But to assume that this is the best or only way to practice tithing is a misrepresentation of one part of a late Hebrew tradition.

Finally, no Christian should conclude from passages in the Hebrew Scripture that tithing in some way demonstrates the complete faithfulness of the believer. Some arguments supporting the tithe from the Hebrew Scriptures, taken out of context, can easily lead the theologian dangerously close to a theology in which the righteousness of God is satisfied but the tithe should never be viewed as the ultimate fulfillment of any person's covenant with God. In many Christian stewardship books on tithing today, one finds strong hints that the practice of offering a tithe to the church sets Christian persons apart from others who do not do so. This interpretation is a misunderstanding of the Hebrew traditions we have examined and is cause for theological concern and caution.

Summary

The tithe is a practice of giving that extends from the covenant relationship. It is a form of sacrifice, of worship in which offering is made to God of something of tremendous value: one's money and one's yearly accumulated goods. In offering God these things, a person enters into a new dimension in their covenant with God. What are some of the elements of this new dimension of life found in the covenant?

In a later chapter, we shall examine these elements more carefully in the context of the daily practice of giving. However, to close this chapter, we can briefly summarize some of the theological elements in the covenant relationship.

First, the offering of a tithe opens a person to a spiritual examination of what is foremost in importance for that person's life. As Israel was challenged to offer a tithe in order to place Yahweh at the center of the community, so the offering of a tithe today makes it possible for a person to consider money second and God first. The spiritual battle for determination of what is most important in one's life is a critical issue for a person's spiritual well-being and growth. It is not possible, for example, to claim we love others if we place ourselves first all the time. The issue of love and support in a relationship toward a significant other requires evaluation of just how important the other really is. In a covenant relationship with God, it is just as important that the partner decide freely how significant God really is. The act of giving one's money away and of offering oneself in a sacrificial financial way is a profound spiritual statement about the authority of God over one's life; it acknowledges a spiritual covenant relationship with God.

Second, the act of offering a tithe creates the opportunity in a person for vulnerability. Without vulnerability there is no risk-taking, and without risk-taking there is no real basis of trust in the covenant with God. Just as Abram and all Israel were vulnerable to Yahweh through the call into covenant and the voluntary offering of the tithe in response, so is any modern person vulnerable who chooses to respond to God in a similar manner.

Third, the act of offering a tithe opens a person to the possibility of learning how to receive. As Israel offered Yahweh the tithe as an act of sacrifice, Israel also became open to receiving the fulfillment of promises made in the covenant. So it is with anyone who chooses to tithe. That person who chooses to tithe is opened to receiving from God whatever God has to offer in return. There is no guarantee that God will offer something that the person desires. To tithe is not to gain some magical power over God so that suddenly God will be required to give us only what we say we want. In fact, what God offers back to us might be far different than what we request. The tithe is not a tool of leverage to be used with the Almighty in order to get one's needs met. The tithe is, rather, a practice of regular giving, leading a person into consequences that develop character and investment in the divine covenant.

In our investigation of the Hebrew concept of the tithe, we have also discovered many problems. Although it is fairly clear why one should consider the practice of the tithe, it is not clear at all how to properly determine what a tithe actually is. This problem we shall leave until the final chapter.

We have also not solved the problem of to whom to give our tithe. The Hebrew Scripture varies on the issue and seems to offer no agreement about the matter. I have tried to show in this chapter that the essential issue of tithing in the Hebrew Scripture is one of faithful offering. However, we shall attempt to provide a solution to this problem as well in our final chapter.

We now turn to Jesus and his theology of stewardship. We turn to Jesus because all Christianity is founded on this one historical figure. Jesus had much to say in his parables about God, about money, and about the covenant. We shall examine the parables in order to determine what Jesus has to say about giving.

CHAPTER THREE

Stewardship and the Parables of Jesus

Jesus knew well the Jewish tradition of the tithe and did not, in fact, object to it. Yet the parables of Jesus contain a radical stewardship theology, which goes far beyond the tithe.

In the last chapter we uncovered a varied and long tradition of giving in ancient Israel. Now we turn to the New Testament in order to discover the impact of the Hebrew tradition on Christianity and on Jesus of Nazareth. One finds very little in the New Testament concerning the tithe. Unfortunately, some modern Christian authors have tended simply to interpret this absence as Jesus' silent affirmation of the tithe tradition. This argument is unpersuasive. Let us turn to the text and tradition to learn what Jesus has to say about stewardship and, in particular, the issue of money.

Introduction to the Jesus Tradition

In the first three Gospels, Jesus is understood as the great rabbi who, with his radical teaching, brings controversy to the Jews of Palestine and salvation to the world. However, the Gospel writers have presented a problem to modern readers. The Jesus that we are offered in the first three Gospels is one of a tradition handed down to the Gospel writers from the early Church in the form of oral and written sources. Since all three of the writers of the first three Gospels are dependant upon this same early Christian tradition, scholars often refer to these Gospels as "synoptic" in nature, or having to do with a similar viewpoint or perspective.

Unfortunately, we do not know very much about the historical Jesus. After all, Jesus was not recorded by microphone or by television cameras. We know of no written materials that Jesus composed. So we only have what has been reported to us by people who may or may not have actually heard Jesus preach. These people, who report the information, were already Christian believers. So we cannot call them independent or impartial in their interpretations of what they possibly saw or heard.

In addition, most scholarly study of the Gospels in this century has concluded that the writers of the synoptic Gospels probably did not have personal knowledge of the historical Jesus. More than likely the Gospel writers depended heavily upon both the written and oral reports they received from other Christians in the early Church.[1]

Scholarly consensus also affirms that what we know about Jesus' historical life is sketchy. However, scholarship in the twentieth century has shown that significant material in the synoptic Gospels may be considered genuine and originating with the historical Jesus. So although we may not know much about Jesus' personal history, we do indeed know a great deal about his teaching.

This knowledge of Jesus' teaching originates directly from statements in the synoptic Gospels that most scholars have accepted as genuine. These genuine sayings, sometimes called *dominical* sayings, consist of various statements and parables. Scholars have argued about the historical value of this material, yet it continues to be accepted and recognized as originating with Jesus of Nazareth. Our study cannot delve into the history or the nature of those scholarly arguments, but notes are provided for readers who wish to learn more.[2]

Suffice it to say here that the general consensus among scholars today is that certain sayings and parables in the first three Gospels are, in the highest probability, those of the historical Jesus.[3] In this chapter, we shall study closely some of Jesus' parables. In the next chapter, we shall study some of Jesus' sayings.

The Parables of Jesus

Our focus in this chapter is upon particular parables of Jesus that are recognized by most scholars as genuine. The purpose of the investigation of this material is to show the origins of stewardship theology in the teaching of Jesus. Our thesis is simple. Jesus knew the Jewish tradition of the tithe well and did not, in fact, object to it. Yet the parables of Jesus contain a radical stewardship theology that goes far beyond the tithe. This stewardship theology is fundamental to the teaching of Jesus and, therefore, must be understood as a necessary element in Christian stewardship thinking and in Christian discipleship.

The History of Parable Research

Research by scholars into the synoptic Gospels in the past one hundred years has yielded a wealth of information about the parables of Jesus. Numerous facts have been learned that now help in the interpretation of the parables, and scholars are learning more each year. A little knowledge of this research will assist in the interpretation of the parables studied in this chapter.

In the nineteenth century, a German scholar named Adolf Julicher offered a major contribution to parable studies. In 1886, Julicher published the first volume of his study *Die Gleichnisreden Jesu*, which traced the history of how the parables of Jesus had been interpreted in Christian history from the period of the early Church to his own time.[4]

Julicher's study produced a startling conclusion. Throughout the long history of Christianity, Julicher could not find any church father who had ever interpreted a parable of Jesus by first asking, How does one properly interpret a first century Jewish parable? Thus, Julicher was forced to conclude *that no one in the history of Christianity had ever interpreted the parables of Jesus properly.*

The parables of Jesus, which are now found in the synoptic Gospels, were originally spoken by Jesus in his native language, Aramaic. However, Jesus' parables were transmitted by the writers of the synoptics only in the *koine* (common) Greek of the first century. Julicher's survey of the various interpretations of the parables in the early Church showed that, assuming the parables were translated properly and accurately by early Christian translators (and we now know that sometimes they were not), the Greek reader of the synoptic Gospels was still left with a problem. Hellenistic culture had no literary tradition of parables similar to that of Judaism. Therefore, reasoned Julicher, the tendency of the Greek writer, using materials translated from the Aramaic original, would be to interpret the parable in a way that a Greek audience could better understand.

Julicher concluded that the result of this tendency to hellenize was that a Gospel writer was probably not aware of how a parable was understood by the Aramaic-speaking audience to whom Jesus of Nazareth delivered it!

The second volume of Julicher's study appeared in 1898 and immediately created a sensation. This volume focused upon the synoptic Gospels. It showed clearly that the Greek translators of the parables and the synoptic writers had, in fact, changed the meaning of the parables by *supplying the parables with allegorical settings or interpretations.*[5] Allegory was a distinctly Greek form of interpretation that developed among Stoic philosophers. It presupposed that the characters in a literary story each had some kind of symbolic or hidden meanings.

Julicher showed in his 1898 study that the Gospel writers all favored allegory as an appropriate method of interpretation for the parables of Jesus. The problem this presented, however, was that Jesus was obviously not Greek, certainly not a Stoic, and probably never intended his parables to be interpreted with the method known among Greeks as allegorical. Julicher, therefore, raised one of the most important questions in New Testament research: If allegorical interpretation is not an appropriate method for the proper understanding of the parables of Jesus, what method is?

The answer Julicher's study offers, and which is still being debated today, is a simple one. A parable is an analogy, a comparison is made between one picture and another. The only way to interpret the analogy properly is to compare the pictures in the parable and see how they fit together. This is probably what Jesus' audience did. They simply compared the images presented in the parable and drew their own conclusions. Julicher argued that the broadest kind of interpretation ought to be given to the comparison process in any parable. By generalizing the interpretation, Julicher reasoned, the parable could become universal in its significance.

Today, the work of Adolf Julicher generally remains unappreciated, available only to readers of German and for the most part unrecognized among Western Protestant Christians. However, it is Julicher who opened a new possibility for all Christians in the West to finally understand the real Jewish character of the historical Jesus and, in particular, the manner in which Jesus used the parable form in his teaching.

For Julicher, Jesus of Nazareth was a simple Jewish rabbinical teacher who used a familiar form, the parable, to teach his message universally.

In 1935 C. H. Dodd, an English scholar influenced by Julicher, published a book entitled *The Parables of the Kingdom.* In this ground-breaking book on parables, Dodd defined a parable as "a metaphor or simile drawn from nature or common life, arresting the hearer by its vividness or strangeness, and leaving the mind in sufficient doubt about its precise application to tease it into active thought."[6]

Dodd further made the point that the parable could only be interpreted properly if it were given one point of comparison that produced a clear meaning congruent with the general dominical sayings of Jesus.[7] In other words, the one proper interpretation of the parable had to be consistent with other information known about Jesus' teaching.

Dodd proposed that the generally correct setting for most of the parables of Jesus had to be taken from the way the parables were introduced. In some cases, the parables of Jesus had no noticeable introductory characteristics. But in many, he noted, the parable was introduced with the statement "The kingdom of God is like." Dodd believed that this introduction was a dominical one originating with the historical Jesus, and therefore provides the proper application of the parable. By *application* Dodd simply meant that the parable had to be interpreted in a way congruent with Jesus' teaching about the kingdom of God. Hence, a parable introduced with the words "The kingdom of God is like" was probably a parable about the kingdom of God itself.[8]

The work of C. H. Dodd still enjoys an enormous following among biblical scholars in the United States and around the world. Advances since the 1940s in parable research have led to more interpretive sophistication, but the framework of Julicher and Dodd still remains fundamental for parable investigation. It is with this framework that our study now begins.

Method

Our method of investigation shall take into account the work of Julicher and Dodd but also incorporate some new elements. First, our study shall include a method of parable interpretation that examines each parable as a series of word pictures. The method we will use to accomplish this task involves an analysis of the structure of those pictures. It is sometimes called structuralism. The method here is a modified type of structural examination by which we will investigate the patterns of the parable story. This analysis of the picture patterns in the parable will be accomplished by creating graphs, which show the parable as a series of word pictures. Then the graphs will help show how the images relate to one another.

Second, our study will attempt to answer the question, What do these parables say, if anything, about the Hebrew stewardship tradition of which Jesus was a part? Since the time of the Protestant Reformation, the general tendency of most study of the Christian Scriptures has been to view the analysis of a biblical text as a theological task that must be brought into relation with traditional doctrinal categories of Protestant thought. Not surprisingly, the issue of stewardship has received little recognition. So our study seeks to determine if something has been missed. We seek to determine if the kingdom parables of Jesus contain significant theological teachings about the topic of stewardship.

Now let us begin our study of some of Jesus' parables. (Translations from the Greek used in this chapter are my own.)

Mark 4:26-29

Jesus said,

> The kingdom of God is as if a man should
> cast seed on the ground. The man sleeps and
> rises, while night and day, the seed springs up
> and grows. The man does not know how.
> The earth brings forth fruit, first the blade,
> then the ear, then the full corn of the ear.
> And when the fruit is ripe, the man puts
> forth the sickle, because harvest time has come.

We begin with this parable for a reason. Few scholars doubt that this parable originated with Jesus of Nazareth. We can see that Mark understands the parable to be about the kingdom of God.[9] This, as Dodd would say, is its application. The parable is intended to say something about the nature of the kingdom.

Before we go any further, we must ask what Jesus might mean by the words *kingdom of God*. Following the lead of Jülicher, we cannot assume that this phrase means something symbolic or allegorical. We must investigate how this phrase might be understood by a first-century Jew.

Obviously, the first place our search for this phrase's meaning must take us is to the Hebrew Scriptures. Any devout first-century Jew, including Jesus himself, would certainly have a very good knowledge of these writings. Not surprisingly, there we find a wealth of tradition concerning the kingdom of God, all of which existed prior to Jesus. Let us now examine some of this tradition.

According to Mic. 2:13, "He who walks at their head will lead the way in front of them; he will walk at their head, they will pass through the gate and go out by it; their king will go on in front of them, Yahweh at their head." Mic. 4:7 speaks of Yahweh's reign as well.

In Zeph. 3:15 we find another reference to the kingdom of Yahweh: "Yahweh has repealed your sentence; he has driven your enemies away. Yahweh, the king of Israel, is in your midst, you have no more evil to fear." And Jer. 3:17 states, "When that time comes, Jerusalem shall be called: The Throne of Yahweh; all the nations will gather there in the name of Yahweh and will no longer follow the dictates of their own stubborn hearts." We find also in Ezek. 20:30: "As I live I swear it—it is the Lord Yahweh who speaks—I am the one who will reign over you." Similar references are found in Isa. 24:23, 43:15, and 52:7. References of interest are also found in Obad. 21 and Zech. 14:9. Most of these references are about the future day when Yahweh will become king of all. They are eschatological, or prophetic promises that look to the future. First-century Jews listening to the parables of Jesus would have been familiar with these prophecies. The first century in Palestine was a time of numerous prophetic or eschatological preachers who warned constantly of the coming end.

Another major tradition of kingship for Yahweh is found in several important Hebrew psalms. Of particular interest are Psalms 47, 93, 96, 97, 98, and 99. These psalms contain the theology of kingship, righteousness, and justice, which fits quite well with the eschatological sayings of Jesus. They contain theology that, as C. H. Dodd would say, fits the application of the parable.[10]

In these psalms, God is portrayed as a king who rules with justice and righteousness. Psalm 98:9 states, "He comes to judge the earth, to judge the world with righteousness and the nations with strict justice." In Ps. 47:7 we find "God is king of the whole world, play your best in his honor!" In Ps. 96:10 we also find "Say among the nations, 'Yahweh is king!' Firm has he made the world, and unshakable; he will judge each nation with strict justice." And finally, in Ps. 97:9 we find "Yahweh loves those who repudiate evil;

he guards the souls of the devout, rescuing them from the clutch-es of the wicked."

No doubt, when Jesus speaks of the kingdom of God, he refers to this tradition in the Psalms and in the Prophets. To be sure, this is the tradition his hearers would have understood him to be talk-ing about. The kingdom of God is set in the context of an ancient covenant that promises that God shall one day reign as a great king in the lives of the people of Israel. The kingdom of God is part of a covenant with God that requires eventual justice and righteous-ness for all. The kingdom of God is eschatological. It will one day come in its fullness, and God will reign over Israel and the rest of the world forever. The parable from Mark's Gospel is about this coming eschatological kingdom of God.

We turn now to the story Jesus presents about the kingdom. Jesus tells us that the kingdom is like a man who plants seed. How can we properly measure what this picture of the man planting seed might mean? By using a graph as described above.[11]

The story is simple, and when it is put on a graph we see some interesting relationships we could not see before. First, there is a man. We know nothing about this man except that he performs several actions. To begin with, he plants seed. This action of plant-ing is represented on the graph by the line drawn from the man to the seed. The work *scatters* appears in the center of the line simply to connote the significance of the verb to its subject and object.

Next, the parable tells us that the man sleeps and rises while the seed is growing. He does not know how the seed grows, but it does grow up into plants. The man comes back into action again when it is time to harvest the plants full of grain. Here again, the line drawn with the word *harvests* on it simply represents the verb action of the man harvesting the plants.

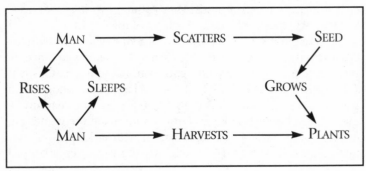

What does this graph tell us about the meaning of the parable? It shows *the comparison of two opposite ironic pictures that lead to the creation of a paradox.* On the one hand, the man sleeps and rises. On the other hand, we are specifically given a picture that the seeds are growing into plants. The irony is that, although the plants grow as a result of this man planting the seed, the man appears to have absolutely nothing to do with the way the seeds have become full-grown plants, nor has he had anything to do with the entire growth process. The paradox is to be found in the comparison of the two pictures: the actions of the man and the growth of the seed.

Other scholars have recognized that paradox is a consistent element present in the parables of Jesus. However, I contend that paradox is present in all of the dominical kingdom parables. I also contend that these paradoxes are interpretive keys for the proper understanding of the kingdom parables. How? Let's complete the interpretation of this parable; then the answer to this question will become more clear.

How is the kingdom of God like a man who plants seed, who sleeps while the seed grows, and who also paradoxically doesn't know how the seed become plants but harvests them anyway? Perhaps asking the question in a little different way, in the context of Israel's covenant relationship, will make the answer a little more obvious. How is the covenant reign of God, when it comes into fulfillment in Israel, like the events in the parable?

Interpretation

The answer is found in the meaning of the paradoxes. The man has no control over what happens in the story except in two obvious points in the parable: planting and harvesting. The rest of the time the man is a passive figure who clearly has no understanding of how the earth produces the harvest. The man plants the seed and harvests after a time of growth. At the heart of the issue is the fact that this man has almost no control over the process of growth of seed into plants. How is the reign of God over Israel like this?

If Israel is to be faithful in covenant with Yahweh, Israel must experience faith as a loss of control over her history. Israel must accept the inclusion of Yahweh's will into her future. Faith also requires the subsequent wait for the outcome of Yahweh's promises.

In this parable, the man gives up something and the man receives something. He gives up control to the process of nature once he plants the seed. Yet, because he is willing to do this in faith, he receives the gift of the harvest from the earth. He does not know how it all works. It just does. Like the seed and its growth, the nature of faith, then, is a willingness to give up control to God and let God reign as covenant king without necessarily knowing the outcome. But this requires a deep sense of trust in God. What makes it even more difficult is that the covenant promise of salvation will be fulfilled for Israel only in the future. There is no apparent reward for faith now. Like the man who waits for the seed to grow so that he may harvest, Israel must wait for Yahweh to fulfill the promises.

This parable's significance in relation to a theology of stewardship is easy to detect. For Jesus, at least in this parable, faith and the kingdom of God are associated with the concept of giving up an old controlled way of life in which people determine their own history. The paradox is that those who gives up their lives to Yahweh receive a new history determined by Yahweh's reign in the covenant. The faithful give up control over their lives and then wait to receive the bidding of Yahweh's will.

To give up control of oneself and to wait to receive from God, in this sense, is to take the paradox of the parable into one's daily life and actually live it. It is to experience the breaking in of the kingdom. In the deepest spiritual sense, *it is to take up a life in faith*.

At its foundation, then, this parable communicates the righteous demand of God that Israel put its faith in Yahweh and in the covenant. It is a call to faith and a call for Israel to surrender her will, her control to God. Hence, for Jesus faith is a willingness to give one's life over to the divine kingship of God. Faith is a willingness to receive direction in history under the guidance of Yahweh.

Mark 4:30-32

Jesus said,

> How shall we speak of the kingdom of God,
> in what parable shall we present it? It is like a
> tiny mustard seed which is smallest among all
> the seeds on earth, but when it is sown upon
> the ground, it grows and becomes the largest
> of garden plants. It puts forth large branches
> so that the birds of the air make their nests
> underneath its shade.

In this parable, the focus once more is upon the comparison of an image from nature with the kingdom of God. Unlike the parable of the seed above, where we are told that the kingdom is like a man who plants seed, the comparison here is with a particular seed planted. This time, moreover, we see other differences. First, the seed is planted, but we are not told by whom.[12] We are only told that the seed is the smallest among seed—a fact that would have been widely known among Aramaic audiences in Palestine. The parable proceeds with the point that the seed grows into a large tree with big branches. Finally, we are told that the branches provide shade in which the birds of the air find likeable places for their nests. The question immediately arises: How is the kingdom of God—the reign of Yahweh—like this?

If we place this parable on a graph, it will appear as follows.

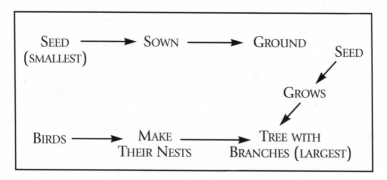

Now, let us attempt to interpret this parable.

First, it is easy to see several paradoxical images placed together in this parable. The most obvious, of course, is that of the smallest seed becomes the largest of trees. More difficult, but just as provocative, is the paradox that from the seed comes a tree used by the birds of Creation. The odd combination of the birds, which generally devour seeds, with the large branches of the tree cannot be foreseen when the seed is planted.

The nature of Israel's faith is similar to the seed. Something must be given to Yahweh before Israel is reconciled to Yahweh and she meets her God. What? As the seed gives itself over to Creation, and then grows, so Israel must give herself over to Yahweh.[13] Israel must give up control of her will in history and begin moving toward the unforeseen consequences of faith. Just as the birds coming to make their nests in the tree is an unforeseen consequence of the seed's growth into a large tree, so encounter with Yahweh's reign as king leads to unforeseen consequences for the faithful. The faithful take up a new direction. The faithful are reconciled to God, and they receive something unexpected from Yahweh. The promises of Yahweh are fulfilled. This process begins only with the radical action of sacrifice, of giving up oneself to Yahweh. Israel must do this soon.

Matt. 13:33

And he spoke to them another parable.

> *The kingdom of heaven is like leaven which*
> *a woman took and mixed into three dry*
> *measures of wheat until it rose up completely.*

The parable of the leaven deals again with the kingdom of God. Here the images are those of wheat and yeast. We are told that the kingdom is like yeast, taken by a woman and mixed into three measures of wheat. The result is that all the wheat rises. If we graph this parable, a picture emerges as follows.

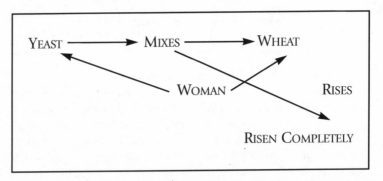

Like the parable of the seed planted by the man (Mark 4:26), this parable contains a human figure, but this time it is the figure of a woman at work. The woman takes yeast and mixes it with wheat. The result is that the wheat and the yeast rise and become dough. A Palestinian would have recognized this process as preparation of wheat meal for bread, eatable except during the Jewish Passover.

More specifically, it is made clear that the kingdom of God is like the yeast added to the meal. The woman is not the focus of the parable. The crux of the comparison appears to be the action of the yeast on the meal. How is the kingdom of God like this? Our graph assists in the answer.

Interpretation

In this parable, the woman initiates the reaction of the yeast and the flour. She is the means through which all significant action takes place, except for the action of the yeast itself. The paradox, however, is that even though she is involved in every aspect of the parable, she herself has nothing to do with the reaction between the flour and yeast which leads to the rising of the dough. The woman does not change, but the wheat and the yeast change into risen dough. The paradox here is that mixing the yeast and the flour produces a foreseen and desired reaction. But the woman, like the man in the parable of the seed in Mark 4:26, is not the cause. The resulting action of the yeasted bread is out of her control.

When the reign of Yahweh comes into the lives of the people of Israel, like the yeast placed in the flour, that reign will produce changes and have consequences for Israel. The key question is whether Israel has the necessary faith. Can Israel put its trust in Yahweh? Like the woman who deliberately put yeast into flour to make bread, Yahweh will thrust judgment upon Israel, and force Israel to choose. Israel must deliberately choose to put her trust in the covenant and all its benefits without controlling or knowing all of Yahweh's divine purposes and will. Like the effect of yeast in wheat flour, the benefits are desirable.

Matt. 13:44

> *The kingdom of heaven is like a treasure hidden*
> *in a field which a man found and hid*
> *again. In great joy he returns home, sells all*
> *that he possesses, and then goes and buys*
> *the same field.*

In this parable, the kingdom is compared to a treasure hidden in a field. Again we see that a man plays a role in the parable. The man discovers the hidden treasure and then buries it again. He returns home, sells all that he possesses, and goes back and buys the field from the owner.

In the graph of this parable, we see the stark contrast, the paradox, between the man's possessions and the man's discovery of the hidden treasure. Note that this parable does not call the possessions of material wealth evil in themselves. Indeed, the choice is between two distinct forms of wealth: the possessions the man has accumulated himself and the possession of buried treasure. Obviously, the treasure is a more valued possession to the man because the man is willing to sell all that he has to gain it.

The second paradox is found in the verbs *buy* and *sell*. On the one hand, the man sells his own possessions, and on the other, he buys property. From the perspective of an outsider, this action seems totally insane. Why sell all that one possesses in order to purchase a piece of undeveloped property? The answer, of course, is that no one else knows what is buried on the property. What do these paradoxes have to do with the kingdom of God?

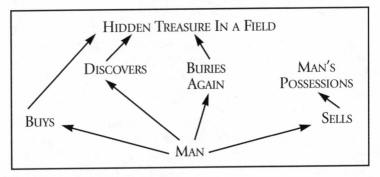

Interpretation

First, the kingdom of God is like a hidden treasure.[14] It is valuable, but its value is hidden in relation to the world. A choice must be made by Israel. Will she choose the world, or will she choose the hidden value of Yahweh's covenant?

Second, choosing the covenant involves sacrifice and a willingness to surrender to Yahweh's will. This act of surrender is seen in the man's willingness to sell all that he possesses to receive the hidden treasure. So Israel must be willing to place Yahweh before the agenda of the world in order to possess the kingdom. Israel must make a choice of priority between the covenant and the securities of this world. The nature of true faith is found in the willingness to choose Yahweh first and sacrifice the agenda of the world.

Matt. 13:45

> *Again, the kingdom of heaven is like a merchant*
> *seeking fine pearls. When he discovers*
> *one pearl of great value, he goes and sells all*
> *that he has and has that pearl.*

This parable appears similar to the parable in Matt. 13:44. Joachim Jeremias, and others, however, have concluded that the two parables are probably from sermons Jesus delivered at separate times. They bear little relation to each other except in form and structure.[15]

In this parable, the kingdom is compared to a man who, acting as a merchant, seeks after fine pearls. Again, we must note that the parable in no way condemns the act of seeking after priceless objects. In fact, the parable is about a man who succeeds in his attempt to do so. The merchant finds one pearl of great value, goes and sells all of his possessions, returns and buys that pearl.

Here we encounter some of the same issues as in the previous parables we have studied. The man is looking for something. What he encounters is far more wonderful than the norm. In this parable, not only does the man find a pearl, but he finds a pearl of unusual value. This unusual situation demands a radical action. The merchant takes radical action, selling all his possessions and purchasing the pearl from its owner.

We can graph this parable in a manner similar to the preceding one. Here, as in the preceding parable, we have the paradox of something of great value over against the possessions accumulated in the normal course of business. The pearl is so valuable and rare that the man decides to purchase it by a radical means. He will sell all that he has to buy it. Again, there is a second paradox, that of finding and buying over against selling. Now we must ask, how is the kingdom of God like a merchant seeking fine pearls?

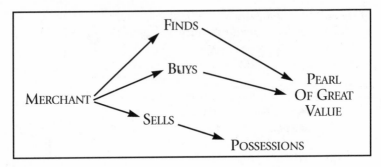

Interpretation

Like the merchant who searches, Israel will not find the riches of Yahweh's kingdom without a desire to seek after them. Israel must seek out Yahweh and then, like the merchant, make a radical choice of faith and turn herself over to Yahweh's coming reign. To make this choice is to sacrifice the value of this world and choose God without guarantee. However, like the merchant who knows the true value of the great pearl and so sells his possessions, Israel knows Yahweh. Through this radical choice, Israel can return to Yahweh in faith and receive her rightful promises. The promises of the covenant will be fulfilled for those who are faithful.

Matt. 20:1-16

> *The kingdom of Heaven is like a vineyard*
> *manager who went out early in the morning*
> *in order to hire workers for the vineyards.*
> *The manager agreed with some workers to go*
> *out and work the entire day in his vineyard*
> *for a denarius. Then, returning at the third*
> *hour, the manager recognized other workers*
> *idle in the marketplace. The manager said to*
> *them, "Get up and go to the vineyards.*
> *Whoever does so, I will give a just wage."*
> *They got up and went into the vineyard to*
> *work. And likewise, again he returned at the*
> *sixth and ninth hours. Near the eleventh*
> *hour he returned again and secured other*
> *workers, and he said to them, "Why do you*
> *stand here idle the whole day?" And they*

> *said to the manager, "Because no one will*
> *hire us." And the manager said to them "Go*
> *also into the vineyard and work." When it became*
> *late in the day, the lord of the manor*
> *came to his manager and said, "Summon the*
> *workers and pay the wages agreed to from the*
> *beginning, paying the last up to the first."*
> *Then those who were hired at the eleventh*
> *hour came forward and received one*
> *denarius. Then came forward those who had*
> *been hired first. Supposing that they would*
> *receive more, they also received one denarius*
> *like the others. But after each took the*
> *denarius, they began to complain to the*
> *manager, saying, "Those men who were hired*
> *last completed only one hour of work, but*
> *you paid them the same as us who bore the*
> *burden and the heat of the day." And the*
> *manager responded to one of them and said,*
> *"Friend, I have not cheated you. Did you not*
> *make a contract with me to work for one*
> *denarius? Now take your things and go. I*
> *want to give the men who came last the same*
> *as I gave to you. Don't I have the right to do*
> *what I wish with My own? Why do you hold*
> *it against me that I am trying to be a*
> *generous man?"*

This parable of the kingdom is more complicated and eventful than the others previously examined. We are told that the kingdom of heaven is like a manager who performs certain actions in the management of the estate over which he has charge. These actions concern the hiring of workers for the master's vineyard. At the beginning of the day, the manager hires by mutual agreement a group of workers at the wage of one denarius. At the third, sixth, and ninth hours, the manager hires other workers and tells them that he will pay them a just wage. Apparently, there is no agreed amount for these workers. Similarly, at the eleventh hour (five o'clock in the afternoon), the manager hires another set of workers. Again, no wage is set for their hour of required work.

At six o'clock in the evening the lord of the manor tells the manager to pay the workers, beginning with those hired last, up to those hired first. The manager does as instructed but, surprisingly, pays all the workers the same amount, the amount agreed upon with those who came first in the hiring process: one denarius.

All those who are under contract for one denarius are angry. They feel that the manager is unfair. They have worked the longest and received the same pay as those who worked only one hour. The manager reminds them that they have a contract and the contract has been fulfilled. Then the manager asks a series of questions to one worker he addresses as "friend." The questions can be summarized as follows: Don't I, as the manager, have the right to pay people not under contract whatever I want to pay them? The only reason offered for his decision to pay these workers the same amount is his wish to be a generous man.

We must ask, how is the kingdom of heaven like this manager and his actions? We can begin to answer this question by placing this parable on a graph.

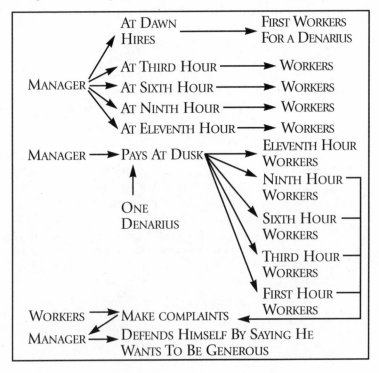

The picture presented to us by the graph is helpful. It shows that the manager in the parable is caught up in three main actions. First, the manager hires workers throughout the day. With the first workers, a special contract is made. Second, the manager pays the workers. The contract is met, and the other workers are paid far more generously than they expect. Third, the manager engages in an argument with the workers under contract.

The contracted workers feel that they are not treated fairly by the manager. They argue that they should receive more than the original contract. They argue this position because they might never have agreed to the contract for one denarius if they had known that the manager intended to pay the other workers one denarius as well. The manager holds the contracted workers to their agreement and simply declares himself to be practicing generosity with the other workers. Thus, the workers who are hired first and under the terms of a safe contract are, technically, paid least for their work. The workers hired last, who have no contract or guarantee, are paid proportionately the most. Paradoxically, those who have the guarantee of a contract feel they have come out the worst in the deal. This is not to mention the fact that the practice of the manager is poor economics and, logically speaking, unexpected.

At the beginning of the parable we are told that the manager needs workers for the vineyard. But when the manager pays the workers, we learn that the reason for giving them the same pay is that the manager wishes to practice generosity. Now we must ask, how is the kingdom of heaven like this?

Interpretation

Just as the manager seeks out workers in the marketplace who must themselves decide if they want to work, so Yahweh is seeking out Israel. The coming of the kingdom requires that Israel make a decision. Will Israel return to Yahweh and live in the covenant, not knowing the recompense that Yahweh will give for Israel's faithfulness? Or, like the workers under contract, will Israel continue to complain and only keep to the covenant's terms as legally binding? Yahweh seeks those who will sacrifice and invest themselves in the covenant by faithfulness. Like the manager, Yahweh is just and righteous to those in the covenant. But Yahweh is also faithful to those who have lost their hope and their trust in Yahweh's justice. Even those who trust Yahweh and do not require guarantees will receive the fulfillment of the promises of the covenant.

Israel is like the parable's contracted workers. She complains to Yahweh about the promised payoff of being in the covenant. Israel never seems satisfied with Yahweh and wants more than she deserves. Like the contracted workers, Israel will be sent away if she does not repent and accept Yahweh's will. Like the manager, Yahweh's will is to be generous. The attitude of faith is not complaint but thankfulness.

Jesus' Theology of Stewardship

In this brief examination of the kingdom of God parables, we have seen the demonstration of certain common characteristics, which can now be summarized and discussed.

First, each parable of Jesus in some way calls Israel to repentance. This call requires a willingness to return to Yahweh and let Yahweh's divine will rule. The call to repentance is a serious and imminent one. Israel must sacrifice her willfulness and return to God in faith with an attitude of thankfulness, now. Why? Because the fulfillment of the kingdom is near.

Second, the parables of Jesus generally reaffirm Yahweh's promises to Israel in the covenant. These promises will be fulfilled in the near future, when Yahweh will reign as king in fullness. Israel will receive her just reward so long as Israel is faithful to the covenant on a day-by-day basis. Israel must rely on Yahweh and seek Yahweh's will. Only this will guarantee the beneficial grace and fulfillment of Yahweh's promises in the covenant.

Third, the kingdom of God will break into the life of Israel in its fullness when Israel is faithful. Thus, faith is the key to the coming of the kingdom. Whenever faith is present in the life of a disciple, it involves the loss of control over one's own history. Israel has not given up control. The nature of faith is, in fact, a willingness to sacrifice and to trust Yahweh. Israel is not willing to do this. The faithful live without necessarily understanding Yahweh's purposes. Israel wants to control the purposes of Yahweh. To live in faith is truly to be under the control of Yahweh and to choose a history compatible with that of Yahweh's will. Sin begins when choices are made that abrogate Yahweh's will. This is Israel's sin. Israel wants to determine her own future and yet still receive the benefits of the covenant.

Fourth, since Yahweh's will is always a just will, if Israel chooses the kingdom, Israel must be willing to live according to Yahweh's justice. Israel is not ready to live justly. Hence, the kingdom will be manifested in judgment and will be given over to those who are willing to live with just behavior.

Finally, although money and the pursuit of money is not condemned, these parables make clear that kingdom values are more important than the values of the world. Unfortunately, Israel has given up on the values of the covenant and turned to guarantees and other worldly values. The promise of Yahweh is that the hidden rewards of the kingdom are greater than any material or monetary rewards. These rewards, however, for the most part, lie in the future and are not readily foreseen in the present.

Discussion

In these parables we see a common theme. Discipleship requires sacrifice and a willingness to receive benefits from God. Thus, in a fundamental sense, sacrifice and acceptance are basic to the teaching of Jesus.

What is the necessary sacrifice? The answer in the parables is quite clear. The necessary sacrifice is that of the self, the surrender of one's will to the will of God. These themes are consistent with Hebrew theology wherein the prophets called upon the people of Israel to sacrifice their old ways and return to Yahweh. In return, Yahweh will fulfill the covenant.

The parables also make clear that faith is more than simple belief in God. Faith is a willingness to turn one's history over to the God of history. It is a willingness to put one's trust in God without necessarily knowing what kind of payoff to expect. In other words, faith has nothing to do with immediate personal reward. In fact, those who give their history over to God may see no reward at all for doing so. Rather, faith invokes a radical disruption of one's self-determination and the intrusion of God's will into the historical process.

Thus, the faithful person is willing to give himself or herself over to God, to wait and see if the promise of reward is fulfilled. This reward, however, need not be something expected. It may be something a person does not expect or even want. It will be the reward chosen by God, not by the faithful person. In this sense, then, faith truly is a sacrifice, and at its foundation, faith contains no elements of magic. For it requires the giving up of oneself to God without any apparent recompense.

For Jesus, like the prophets before him, the journey into faith begins with a decision to give oneself over to God totally. Making this decision begins with a series of sacrifices. We find echoes of this call for sacrifice in other dominical sayings of Jesus. The more one sacrifices, the more one places one's trust in the hands of God. Sacrifice, then, is a key to beginning the journey of faith.

For Jesus, receiving the kingdom is the result of a willingness to sacrifice one's history in faith. Receiving the kingdom means that God draws near and that the reign of God begins to break into one's life. Receiving is a fundamental element in the fulfillment of the promises of God. Receiving permits God's will to function in a disciple's life. Through receiving, the history of a person is molded by God. Thus, accepting what is given by God to one in the covenant is a major theme in Jesus' theology.

For Jesus, when the kingdom breaks into a person's life, the behavior of that person must be just because that person's will comes under the force of the just, divine will of God. Injustice is never compatible with the in-breaking of the kingdom of God.

Jesus and Stewardship

Stewardship, then, for Jesus, is at the heart of faith and his teaching on the kingdom of God. He portrays it as an exchange of gifts between God and humankind in the covenant. The steward must also live in the covenant relationship with God according to the moral values of the divine will. These values include the steward's willingness to undergo ethical evaluation and judgment by God and a willingness to revolutionize one's ethical and moral actions. Thus, for Jesus, and for the modern disciple, a life in faith contains a radical element. It is the constant demand of God upon the disciple to sacrifice one's life to God and to receive from God the new direction of the divine will as well. Without this constant willingness to exchange sacrifice for grace, the follower becomes a wanderer through history.

CHAPTER FOUR

The Tithe in the New Testament

The question immediately arises, why are there no clear and significant references to tithing in the New Testament?

We have seen in our study so far that an important theological tradition of stewardship existed in the Hebrew Scriptures. We have also seen that Jesus, at least in his parables of the kingdom, indirectly draws upon that same tradition. However, some significant differences remain. While the Hebrew stewardship tradition focuses upon the tithe and its practice in relation to the covenant, Jesus focuses more upon the eschatological judgment of Israel and calls upon Israel to return to the covenant and to attain to the kingdom of God.

We have also seen that Jesus never condemns money in his kingdom parables. This raises an important issue in the synoptic tradition, where Jesus is constantly portrayed by the Gospel writers as opposed to the rich and to money. Why do the parables not condemn money and the rich, while the later tradition found in Matthew, Mark, and Luke is critical of people who have or seek after money? And what about the tithe?

Curiously, the synoptic tradition of Matthew, Mark, and Luke contains little about the tithe.[1] For many Christians who have studied the tithe, this has been a tremendous problem. After all, if tithing is affirmed by the Hebrew Scriptures but generally ignored in the Gospels and the remainder of the New Testament, what is a Christian to do in his or her practice of giving to the church? What models exist for Christian giving in the New Testament, and how does the tithe relate to these models? In this chapter, we shall explore these questions and attempt to offer some answers.

Introduction to the Synoptic Gospels

Scholarship investigating the New Testament in the last one hundred years has uncovered some important facts about the construction of the Gospels as well as the other early material in the Christian canon. For our investigation we must know what scholars have commonly accepted about the development of the Gospels.

First, it has become accepted almost universally among scholars today that the synoptic Gospels were written by a process of collecting and compiling oral and written traditions. The writers received traditions from the communities in which they lived and practiced their faith. Thus, we now know that more than likely both the communal and the personal faith of each Gospel writer has highly influenced and shaped the construction of each Gospel. Also most New Testament scholars accept that both Matthew and Luke were constructed with the help of two written sources. Both writers apparently had copies of the Gospel of Mark in front of them. Mark is more than likely the literary model for both Matthew and Luke, and it is most probably the earliest written Gospel of the three.[2]

Second, scholars now generally accept the view that the other written source used by Matthew and Luke was probably a copy of a document that contained sayings of Jesus and certain other very old eschatological material. Modern scholars refer to this written source document by the name Q. This is an abbreviation for the German word *Quelle*, which means "source."[3]

The Q document is now believed lost and unavailable to modern researchers. So we cannot know exactly what sayings and materials the document contained. However, we can detect some traces of Q in Matthew and Luke by comparing passages in the two that are almost word-for-word alike in structure and meaning but that do not appear in the Gospel of Mark. Scholars generally now agree that Q probably can be dated in the late forties or early fifties of the first century. Q is, therefore, a written document roughly contemporary with the genuine letters of Paul.

Scholars also believe that Matthew and Luke probably had other oral traditions and sources available for their use in the construction of their Gospels. Scholars sometimes label these oral sources M and L respectively. Whether the oral material in M and L is as old as Q is still debated. However, by means of critical study, M and L can be detected, and each source offers important clues to the construction of each Gospel. For example, it is possible to study material from *M* in Matthew and from this material begin to determine some of Matthew's particular feelings and views about life and faith in his Christian community. The same is true of a study of *L*. Understanding these views is quite helpful for a better comprehension of each Gospel writer's particular theo-logical purpose.

The Q Document

With regard to the issue of stewardship and, in particular, the issue of the stewardship of money, the *Q* document contains some sayings from Jesus that demonstrate a very interesting difference from the message outlined earlier in our study of Jesus' kingdom parables. In the *Q* document, Jesus is an eschatological teacher for whom the end of the world is near. Therefore, the pursuit of money is, practically speaking, viewed as a foolish and useless concern. Indeed, the sayings in *Q* set the importance of money and wealth over against God's imminent reign.

As we have already seen in the examination of the kingdom parables, Jesus actually uses images of people pursuing wealth to make a number of theological points about faith and God's divine kingship. According to Jesus in many of these parables, faith is a giving up of one's control to Yahweh's divine will and a willingness to serve and be guided by Yahweh in history. One does not see in Jesus' kingdom parables a rejection of wealth per se, nor do we detect Jesus placing wealth over against faith in God. Let us now examine a few examples of *Q* sayings.

In Matt. 6: 19-21, we find a quotation from *Q* in which Jesus states:

> *Do not collect treasure for yourselves on*
> *earth where corrosion and moth can disfigure*
> *it and where thieves can break in and steal it.*
> *But rather gather up treasure in heaven,*
> *where neither moth nor corrosion bother it,*
> *and where thieves can neither break in nor*
> *steal it. For where your treasure is, there*
> *will be your heart also.*

Another quotation from *Q* follows in Matt. 6:24:

> *No man can become a servant for two lords.*
> *For he will either hate the one and love the*
> *other, or he will be loyal to the first, and*
> *despise the second. You cannot serve God*
> *and Money at the same time.*

First, we can see that these quotations contain a negative view of money and of the world: the values of the world are less important to Jesus than the coming kingdom. Money, and those who pursue money, are condemned. Certainly in these passages we see the viewpoint that there is no spiritual benefit for those who choose to make money the most important factor in their existence. The Jesus of the parables apparently makes no effort to condemn money or those pursuing money, but the Jesus of Q introduces the spiritual division of those who have money and those who do not. On the one hand stand God and treasures in heaven, and on the other stands the world filled with things that have no inherent value for spiritual life.

In another parable in Q, the Parable of the Talents (Matt. 25:14-30 and Luke 19:11 - 27), we can detect where the Q editor diverges from the Jesus tradition. The parable concerns servants who are each given a large amount of money—a talent. The master who gives the servants money wishes for each to manage it in his own way. The master then leaves the country for a journey.

While the master is gone, the servants take the money entrusted to them and some generate more. When the master returns, all who have increased their number of talents are rewarded. One servant, however, who simply hides his talent in the ground and returns it to the master, is punished.

There is no question that the parable is consistent in structure and content with other parables we have examined. Like the kingdom parables, it illustrates an important teaching of Jesus. Israel must take what she has been given by Yahweh in the covenant and use it, now, before God gives the covenant and its benefits to others. The parable obviously praises the economic gain of the servants who do, in fact, use their talents to gain more for the master, and it condemns the servant who is frightened and lazy. The point of our observations, however, is that the Q editor has understood the parable in another way. For the Q writer, the parable is a warning of the coming end for those who do not prepare to meet the coming King by giving away their possessions.

Jesus the Jew communicated that the things of the world are there to be managed and used judiciously for the coming reign of God's kingdom. But it is highly unlikely that Jesus would have viewed money and possessions as evil to the extent recorded in Q. In fact, we have seen this in our study of Jesus' parables. The Jesus of the parables, like the Jesus in this Parable of the Talents, is simply not interested in condemning money or wealth. It must be concluded that *the Q editor had some special interest in condemning those who focus on the attainment of money and worldly goods.*

It is evident that just like the later Gospel writers, the compiler of the Q document must be considered an editor with theological interests and purposes that affect the Jesus tradition. For the Q editor, Jesus is an eschatological teacher who clearly manifests an other-worldly character and teaching. Material things, money, and the pursuit of worldly monetary success are viewed as interfering with the Q community's spiritual pursuit of God's reign on earth. This view, without doubt, represents an overall Hellenistic or Greek tendency, setting the spiritual world against the material. This tendency can, and in this case does, result in a theological dualism in which money and possessions are pitted against the kingdom and God.

Mark

If the writer of the Gospel of Mark does not know the Q document, as most biblical scholars currently believe, then we can say that the dualistic demand that sets radical faithfulness to Jesus against money must be an important value and viewpoint in the early stages of the synoptic tradition—for Mark holds many of the same views as Q on the subject. Let us begin our survey of Mark by considering several relevant passages.

In Mark 6:7-13 we find the story of Jesus sending out the Twelve on a mission into the villages and towns of Palestine. The instructions to the Twelve, reported by Mark, indicate Mark's attitude concerning apostolic ministry.

> *And he instructed them to take nothing on*
> *the road except a lone staff—no bread, no*
> *beggar's bag, no copper coins in their money*
> *belts—to put on sandals, but not to wear two*
> *tunics. And he said to them, "When you*

> enter someone's home, stay there until you
> leave that place. And if someone in that
> place will not receive or listen to you,
> when you leave that place, shake the dust off of
> your feet as a witness to them."

This passage is quite representative of Mark. Mark begins by reporting what the disciples are to wear on their journey and what preparations they are to make. However, Mark does not give us the direct quotation from Jesus concerning these preparations. When Mark does quote Jesus, Jesus simply states that if the disciples are welcomed by hospitable Jews, they are to stay in that friendly house until they leave the area. If they are not welcomed, they are to practice the prophetic Jewish symbol of judgment by shaking off the dust from their feet in front of that house. In other words, Jesus tells the disciples to take advantage of the Jewish hospitality law, which requires the Jewish community to welcome strangers and to provide food and housing for them.

One conclusion we can draw from this passage is that Mark wants to make clear to all his readers that absolute poverty is Jesus' community's rule for apostolic mission. Similarly to Q, Mark is concerned that the disciples appear to make the ultimate sacrifice by obeying Jesus and going out into the world without financial support as preachers and teachers of the kingdom. Their only means of survival is to accept the willing hospitality of local Jews.

This picture presented by Mark implies that faith is grounded in radical sacrifice. To follow Jesus, one surrenders all and goes into the mission field without any solid means of financial support. For Mark, the willingness to lose control of one's will for the Divine One has become an apostolic model of willingness to live without daily personal provision.

This interpretation is confirmed in the tenth chapter of Mark, where several statements are put forward by Mark concerning wealth versus faith. In Mark 10:17-22 we are told of the confrontation of Jesus with the rich young man.

> And as he began to set out on a journey a
> man came up to Jesus and knelt down before
> him and asked, "Good teacher, what must I
> do to receive the gift of eternal life?" And

> *Jesus said to him, "Why do you call me good?*
> *No one is good except God alone. You know*
> *the commandments. 'Do not commit murder;*
> *do not commit adultery; do not steal; do not*
> *bear false witness; do not cheat another;*
> *honor your father and your mother.' " And the*
> *man responded, "Teacher, I have kept all*
> *these commandments from my youth." And*
> *Jesus, looking upon him, felt great affection*
> *for him and said, "You lack only one thing.*
> *Go and sell all your possessions, give the*
> *money to the needy, and you shall have*
> *treasure in heaven, and come follow me. At*
> *these words, the man's face fell into sadness,*
> *and he went away in great unhappiness; for*
> *he was a very rich man.*

The rich young man says he wants to have eternal life. Jesus replies that the man has done all but one thing to attain it. He must sell all that he has, give the money to the poor, and follow Jesus.

For Mark, the issue is clear. It is not possible to possess wealth, or the comforts of wealth, and also follow Jesus. Faith requires an act of personal sacrifice, a surrender of one's personal wealth. For Mark, this is the ultimate act of faith, that a follower of Jesus would be willing to lay down his or her possessions for the Lord. Mark understands this as the road to Christian perfection; it is the model of the apostles.

If the encounter of the rich young man does not make his position clear enough, Mark attempts to make us certain of his meaning in the next few verses of chapter 10. Most interesting is the fact that these passages present a problem for interpretation. In Mark 10:23-27 we find further confirmation of Mark's view that wealth is incompatible with the kingdom. Here Jesus says, "How difficult it is for the wealthy to enter the kingdom of God" (v.23). Then, after an exchange with the disciples, Jesus says further on, "It is more difficult for a camel to go through the eye of a needle than for a rich man to enter the kingdom of God" (v.25).

There follows an interesting exchange between Jesus and the disciples. The disciples are apparently startled, and they ask, among themselves, "Who then can be saved?" Jesus' response is an important one. "For human beings it is impossible, but not so for God. For all things are possible with God" (v.27). Obviously, this response conflicts with Jesus' opening statement about the rich. If it is as hard for a rich person to get into the kingdom of God as it is for a camel to go through the eye of a needle, certainly no rich person is going into the kingdom. Yet Mark concludes this daring pronouncement by splicing into it another statement of Jesus that creates a paradox: All things are possible for God—even saving the rich! The two incompatible viewpoints appear alongside each other. The apparent meaning of this combination of opposites is that the rich are hard pressed to enter the kingdom, but it is possible under one clear condition: God's mercy.

It is highly likely that these two conflicting statements of Jesus were originally separate and unrelated.[4] For Mark, they are concerned with the meaning of divine judgment and divine grace. The rich man seeks perfection but falls under judgment because he is unwilling to surrender his personhood and his will to God. He wants a procedure, but it is one that requires sacrifice and surrender. It therefore involves faith. The young man is not able to accept the procedure. The result is judgment.

Similarly, the point of the passage about the eye of the needle is that the grace of Yahweh is infinite and not subject to the limitations of human judgment. Grace makes many things possible that do not appear to be so for human beings. Thus, by splicing these passages together, Mark presents the mercy of God as the only hope for the rich. Only those wealthy who throw themselves before God's judgment seat and seek God's infinite mercy can be saved from condemnation.

Matthew

It will come as no surprise that since Matthew is a Gospel constructed with the use of Mark and also with the Q document source, Matthew is consistent with the synoptic tradition's tendency to set money against the kingdom of God. However, some passages from the M source, Matthew's own oral source, show that Matthew sometimes modulates this antagonism between money and the kingdom.

The best example of this is found in parables from the M source, particularly Matt.13:44; 13:45-46, and 20:1-16. Obviously these parables, which we studied above, show little or no such antagonism.

Presumably, Matthew simply placed these parables in his Gospel with little or no change. If so, they show some degree of unwillingness on Matthew's part to reformulate parables about the kingdom. They also reveal that Matthew bends the synoptic tradition just a little for those who have wealth.

The willingness to bend is even more pronounced in Matthew's reproduction of the Q material. For example, in the Sermon on the Mount, Matthew reports Jesus saying, "Blessed are the poor in spirit, for theirs is the kingdom of heaven (5:3)." This quotation is from Q. In Luke's version, we find simply "Blessed are the poor (6:20)." For Matthew, the rich *can* be included among those who are poor *in spirit*. So Matthew makes a little room for the rich, but not very much.

Luke/Acts

The Gospel of Luke and the Book of Acts were both written by the same author and probably with a connected purpose. On the theology of stewardship, we find that Luke carries the tendency of the synoptic tradition to its logical extreme. In both documents money is considered to be on the same spiritual level as Satan.

In Luke 8:2-3 we find Luke's description of the source of livelihood of Jesus and the disciples.

> *And (with Jesus) were some women from whom demons and infirmities had been cast out: Mary, called Magdala, from whom seven demons had been cast out, Joanna, the wife of Chuza, a manager in Herod's household, Susanna, and many other women who provided for them out of their own resources.*

Luke tells us that Jesus and the disciples lived without money or means. During their apostolic ministry, these women provided for their needs.

In other words, the model of apostolic ministry is that of poverty. Luke apparently believes that the apostolic band lives without knowledge of how the next meal will be provided (Luke 9:2-5). Obviously, Luke associates poverty with the radical call of Jesus for faithfulness to the kingdom ideal.

This viewpoint is confirmed in the Book of Acts, where Luke's view of the common life of the early Christian community is described in detail. In Acts 2:44-47, we are told by Luke that the early Christians in Jerusalem held all things in common and shared with each other according to need. For Luke, this Christian lifestyle of holding things in common is absolutely essential. It is the main sign of the reality that all are one in the community. Acts 4:3-37 and 5:1-11 outline most clearly the contrast between those who hold all things in common to those who do not. We are told in Acts 4:32ff that the community held all things in common and that all kinds of needs were met. Believers sold all that they had and brought the proceeds to the apostles, who distributed it to the members.

In Acts 5, Luke offers the reader a strong contrast to this picture of harmony. In the story of Ananias and Sapphira, we are told what happens when someone pretends to give all the proceeds from the sale of their possessions to the apostles. Ananias holds back some of the money from the sale. The result of this deception is that both he and his wife die at the feet of the Apostle Peter. It is obvious from the way the passage is written that both Ananias and Sapphira die because Luke sees their action as a lie to the Holy Spirit. But, of course, the passage also clearly implies that if they had not loved money so much and withheld it from the apostles, their fate would have been different.

Thus, for Luke, money and the spiritual life of the kingdom are totally incompatible. There is no reason for one to keep one's money. It should all be given to the community in order to demonstrate one's spirituality and one's sincere faith in God.

Summary of Synoptic Theology

We see from our survey of Q and the synoptic Gospels that the theology of stewardship originating in the kingdom parables of Jesus is completely transformed in this early Christian literature. For Q and for the Gospel writers, the message of Jesus is that money is a temptation opposing the kingship of God. No one ought to spend time accumulating wealth, because the final consummation is near. God will come soon and reign as king. Thus, the pursuit of wealth is foolish and spiritually destructive.

Jesus' understanding of faith as a loss of control has been totally transformed in the synoptic tradition. For Q and for the Gospel writers, faith is the complete willingness of a person to give control of their lives to God by willingly surrendering all financial claim in the world. One's only claim for food and clothing can be made either to the Christian community or to God, who will provide through people appointed for such purposes.

Paul's Theology of Stewardship

Now we need to turn to another early tradition in the New Testament, that of the Apostle Paul. Paul's genuine letters offer the investigator another insight into a different branch of the early Christian community.[5] Most scholars today date the genuine letters of Paul between the years A.D. 49 and 60. This makes them roughly contemporary with Q and with the early formation period of the synoptic tradition. However, most scholars believe that Paul influenced the synoptic tradition very little. It also appears that the synoptic tradition had little impact on Paul. With these factors in mind, we can now investigate this tradition for another perspective on how the Jesus tradition has been interpreted.

2 Thessalonians

For Paul, money is not in itself evil. In fact, money is to be accumulated by means of honest work (Thess. 3:6-13). The question for all followers of Christ is the right and proper use of one's money. Therefore, a theology of giving is necessary in Paul's teaching, since members of Paul's church are permitted to keep the money they earn. This teaching can be summarized by examining other significant passages in Paul's theology.

1 Corinthians

In the First Letter to the Corinthians, we find that Paul is theologically different from his contemporary Q in his approach to the issue of money and salvation. For Paul, salvation is a gift bestowed by God on whoever will receive it (1 Cor. 2:10-14). The person who receives the gift of salvation and all its mysteries also becomes a steward of the gift (1 Cor. 4:1-2). For Paul, the kingdom of God is manifested in power (1 Cor. 4:20). Thus, whoever receives the gift of the Spirit is empowered by God with spiritual gifts in great variety (1 Cor.12:4-11).

Philippians

In Philippians, Paul makes it clear that the Incarnation was God in Jesus Christ taking on the form of a servant and being emptied out (Phil. 2:4-11). This view is of interest because it echoes the notion found in the parables that the nature of faith evokes willingness to lose one's personal history to Yahweh. Just as Christ has poured himself out by submitting his will to the divine will and has become a servant to God, so the person who would receive the stewardship of the Holy Spirit must be willing to do the same. For Paul, the act of pouring oneself out for God is directly linked to the personal sacrifice of Jesus in another reference as well (Phil. 3:7-11). Hence, for Paul, the offering of oneself sacrificially is a spiritual key to receiving the mysteries of God and, therefore, the way to become a steward of God's salvation.

2 Corinthians

In 2 Corinthians, Paul deals directly with the issue of money and giving. The passages in question are particularly concerned with the collection of money for the saints (9:1ff). For Paul, the infusion of the Holy Spirit into a person's life ultimately causes one to come under the direct control of Christ (5:14), and like Christ, that person who is in the Spirit becomes a giver whose generosity matches the pouring out of Christ himself (8:9). For Paul, giving is not to be accomplished under compulsion (9:7). Rather, giving is linked by Paul to a Hebrew theology of blessing. The more a person gives, the more that person is blessed. The basis of Christian giving is, therefore, love for God and a desire for blessing (8:8-9; 9:6-10).

For Paul, one gives in order to accomplish two objectives. First, one gives to become emptied out like Christ. As a result of this emptying, that person is filled with spiritual gifts and manifestations of the Spirit. Second, one gives to bless others and, therefore, ultimately to be blessed by God's outpouring of gifts. The result of this pilgrimage into giving is an increased understanding of thankfulness for a deepening love of God (2 Cor. 9:12).

Summary of Paul's View

Thus, for Paul, Christian giving is linked to salvation in that an actual exchange occurs between God and humankind through the action of giving, receiving, and God's blessing. This interaction, which Paul sees as the economy of God's household, is directly understood to have a real presence in the lives of Christians who are practicing the imitation of Christ by pouring themselves out and by receiving spiritual gifts and blessings from God.

It is important to note that Paul offers no standard of giving. For Paul, giving is linked to love and to joy. Since there are no limits to the love and joy the community of faith can experience in Christ, there are also no standards for giving oneself or one's money away.

In this sense, then, Paul appears to have understood the parables of Jesus better than editors in the synoptic tradition. Giving is a part of salvation, just as receiving is a part of it, too. For Paul, the salvation process follows the model of the Jewish covenant, but it is expressed in highly Hellenistic terminology.

Christian Giving

With our examination of how Jesus' teaching on covenant evolved in the early Church complete, we can now turn to answering the questions put forward at the beginning of this chapter.

Let us begin with the tithe. Why is the tithe not discussed openly in the New Testament? References to it are rare. Indeed, the word *tithe* is used in only four references: Luke 11:42; Luke 18:12; Matt. 23:23-24; and Heb. 7:5-9. The reference in each of these cases is almost completely indirect and offhand. Only in Hebrews is reference made to the tithes of Levi and the tithes of the new high priest, Melchizedek. These references are vague at best and unhelpful for a theological foundation of Christian tithing.

The question immediately arises, why does the New Testament contain no clear and significant references to tithing? Our examination suggests two reasons. First, the notion of giving a tenth of all that one earns each year to the Christian community is superseded in the synoptic tradition by the view that money is basically evil and unnecessary. The real Christian follower must be willing to radically dispose of any possessions or money by giving them to the church. Just as Jesus and the disciples gave up their money completely, so the faithful Christian must do the same. For anyone who is willing to make Jesus the most important factor in their lives, this is a sign of otherworldliness and faithfulness.

Second, Christians in the Pauline tradition are taught that

money is to be given away by only one standard: a loving desire to help others and to be blessed. For Paul, there is no standard or minimum of giving.

Hence, in Pauline communities, Christian community members are encouraged to work and keep their money. For Paul, true giving can occur only when what is given belongs to the person who gives. Moreover, the possession of money, while not wrong in itself, is ideally for the work of generosity and the spread of the gospel message. There is to be no limit placed on the generosity of the giver. Persons who give generously, in Paul's teaching, pour out their resources for others according to their measure of faith. Thus the ultimate purpose of giving is not to fulfill what is understood as a standard, but rather to bless others and thereby to be blessed by God. Since giving is not to be accomplished by compulsion, the sole standard of the tithe as a mechanical fulfillment of obligation to God is incompatible with Paul's doctrine of giving. This is why we do not find Paul in his letters recommending the tithe as a formal practice of giving.

Discussion

We can see that Christians have several theological models for giving money away. These models are based upon the Hebrew Scripture and the writings of the New Testament. These models of giving can now be summarized.

The Hebrew Model of the Tithe

The first model is found in the Hebrew tradition of the tithe, in which one tenth of one's income is offered to God as a response to the covenant. In this model, the Christian is expected to earn a living by making money as a productive member of an economic community. Money is to be used wisely, and in itself money is neither good nor evil. In this model, the giver must set aside one tenth of his or her total income for each year as an offering to God. This money can be paid to the sacred sanctuary, the clergy, or to the relief of the poor and the needy. The Hebrew tradition clearly permits all of these groups to receive part or all of the tithe. Gifts of money for the construction of the sacred places of God are considered offerings in addition to the tithe. These additional voluntary gifts are based on need and on spontaneous openhandedness. They are not regular offerings made each year to the sanctuary.

The Synoptic Gospel Model

The second model for giving is found in the New Testament synoptic tradition. This tradition makes clear that the possession of money is incompatible with the message of salvation in the context of gospel discipleship. Those who take time to make money for themselves and participate in the worldly economy are able to attain salvation only through the ultimate mercy of God. Clearly, however, even God's mercy has little to offer those who are unjust and rich. But those who voluntarily offer all their money to the community are viewed as faithful, with a secure place in the coming kingdom of God. In Christianity after the New Testament, this model of giving found its true place in the various monastic orders whose members voluntarily took vows of poverty. Of course, many today still follow this radical model of Christian life.

The Pauline Model

The third and final model for giving in the New Testament is found in the genuine letters of the Apostle Paul. For Paul, giving is linked to love for God, to blessing, and to salvation. Giving should not be compulsive or limited by some arbitrary standard like the tithe. Thus, for Paul, Christian giving is linked to personal spiritual growth. He also considered it an open and clear statement of one's faith, displaying a willingness to imitate Jesus and pour oneself out for God's work in the world.

In the Pauline model, like that of the Hebrew Scriptures, neither the accumulation of money nor one's participation in the world's economy is condemned. Like the Hebrew model, Paul emphasizes the proper use of resources in relation to one's faith. Faithful use of them serves to deepen one's commitment to God. Ultimately, in this Pauline model, the tithe is not sacrificial enough. For Paul, generous giving begins when the Christian pours out his or her money as an act of love and faith in response to God's gift of salvation in Jesus Christ. To give very little or to give only the minimum of a tithe would be counter to all the principles of Christ's saving grace. In this model, the tithe was more than likely viewed as a kind of minimum standard that Jews have followed to satisfy the Law. Paul suggests that only sacrificial giving in the name of Jesus Christ lives up to the highest meaning of sacrifice as defined by the life and death of Jesus Christ.

Why Tithe?

Again, we return to the question of why a Christian person should seriously consider giving away one tenth of their income. The answer appears to be this: *Christians who tithe do so in order to fulfill the minimum biblical standard of giving.* Paul states that giving ought to be according to one's love for God and not by compulsion. Nevertheless, Paul states this view in the context of the Jewish practice of the tithe, on the one hand, and some knowledge of the apostolic model of complete surrender of one's money to the Christian community on the other (1 Cor. 9:1-18). Certainly, Paul would never have accepted the practice of not giving at all to the church or of giving less than the Jews gave to the Temple. In fact, the tithe is the minimum standard to which Paul appeals as a foundation for significant, Christian, sacrificial giving in his community. In contrast, the synoptics urge complete surrender of all assets to the Christian community. But this complete surrender of wealth is compulsory. For Paul, Christian giving is integrally linked to spirituality in the salvation process, and it is an extension of faithfulness. Thus, as one's faith and spirituality grow, so grows one's love for God and for giving generously.

Without doubt, for the average American working person interested in promoting their faith and supporting their church, the Pauline model offers the most spiritual and helpful guidance for Christian growth and practice. This practice is simply to give one's money away, the goal being to exceed the tithe and in order to attain a sacrificial out-pouring of oneself in faithful gratitude to God.

Tithe to Whom?

Next we return to the question of to whom the tithe should be directed. For Paul, giving is best directed to the needs of the church. However, it must also be remembered that for Paul the church included the needy saints in Palestine nearby as well as the mission work in faraway places. In many ways, Paul is faithful to his Jewish training on this issue, for he tends to support the guidelines of the Hebrew Scriptures.

Thus, we may summarize our answer to the question as follows. A tithe may be designated for or partially offered to any of the following recipients:

- The local congregation

- The minister's discretionary fund

- Reputable relief funds for the needy

- Reputable organizations that further the world-wide work of the Church

- Other charities that help the needy

Conclusion

On a practical level, this general theological explanation does not resolve the problem of how to tithe. Moreover, to whom one offers the tithe is an important issue which requires further discussion and some practical guidelines. One thing, however, is clear: The Church is the recipient of three very different models of giving that in many ways conflict with each other in both theology and in practice. No wonder the issue of tithing and fund raising have long been at odds with each other; for the Scriptures permit so many ways to raise money for the work of God in the world.

In Part 2 of our study, we turn to the more practical issues of how to apply the Pauline model to one's daily life in the church and in the world.

PART TWO

Stewardship and the
Practice of the Tithe

CHAPTER FIVE

The Tithe and Personal Budgets—
How It All Works

Giving is the first thing a steward must consider in the formulation of his or her budget. Why? Otherwise, the budget will simply reflect a philosophy of offering to God whatever is left over.

We now turn to the practical issues of giving. We must consider some guidelines for tithing in the context of an overall financial plan. We are all creatures of the world as well as Christians pursuing our spirituality and faith in Jesus Christ. For this reason, we will begin our discussion with what it means to be an "economic" person in the world.

Every month or week, each worker or owner of a business receives a stipend for living purposes. For some workers, this stipend is called *payroll*; for others, it is called *salary*. Whatever it is called, this stipend is the means through which each person lives economically in the world. For the Christian steward this stipend raises some important issues. What planning or strategy should one have for the spending of one's money? Does the spending of one's money include a budget in which saving some part of one's income is a priority? Can the budget take into account unforeseen needs and expenses that are a common part of everyday life? How does a person's faith in Jesus Christ and a desire to give sacrificially by tithing (or by exceeding the tithe) relate to the formulation of a budget?

For the Christian steward, a proper consideration and response to these questions falls into six critical financial areas: faithful, sacrificial giving; debt; savings; daily expenses; long-range retirement planning; and the proper preparation for one's death.

Faithful, Sacrificial Giving

In modern America, the notion of constructing a personal budget for one's daily expenses appears to be unpopular. Consumerism and spending in response to business marketing seem to have won the day. However, a person interested in living as a Christian steward must be willing to do the work necessary to budget and manage wisely. The steward accomplishes this goal by developing a financial philosophy and a budget framework for generous giving and financial security.

The Tithe Comes First

Giving is the first thing a steward must consider in the formulation of his or her budget. Why? Otherwise, the budget will simply reflect a philosophy of offering to God whatever is left over after one's own personal needs are met. This may seem a strange and unnatural way to budget. But herein lies an indication of one's highest priority. We have seen in the Hebrew Scriptures that the tithe is understood as an offering to God in response to the covenant. We have also seen that the Hebrew Scriptures, the Gospels, and the parables of Jesus always challenge the faithful person to place God at the center of their lives. In this sense, then, the act of offering one's tithe and other financial gifts to God first in one's budget is a constant spiritual fulfillment of this demand and a reminder that God, not money, is the foundation of one's life.

To place the tithe first in one's budget also makes a statement about one's own management practices. That is, faithful stewards openly declare to God and to others that they can, in fact, live on 90 percent of their income. They acknowledge that they can manage the amount left over after giving sacrificially—and manage it well.

Tithe to Whom?

To whom is this budgeted tithe to be given? We have seen that the Hebrew Scriptures offer a variety of options, including the sanctuary, the clergy, the poor and the needy. We have seen that for Paul the Christian's offering is made to meet the needs of the Church, both locally and throughout the Church's mission field in the world. Hence, I would offer the following guidelines for the practice of tithing and sacrificial giving.

1. Part of one's tithe can be given in regular weekly offerings to one's local congregation or place of worship.

2. Part of one's tithe can be given to reputable organizations in or outside the Church that directly aid the poor and the needy.

3. Part of one's tithe can be offered for the discretionary use of the clergy.

4. Part of one's tithe can be offered to the greater work of the Church, beyond the local congregation in order to help others. This includes offerings toward missionary work throughout the world.

Remembering that the tithe is a kind of minimum biblical standard of giving for all Christians, all of these are proper and biblically sound recipients of financial support. The amount or percentage of money to be given to each must be calculated by thought and prayerful determination. As we have already noted, no rules are set down in either the New Testament or Hebrew Scriptures for a proper determination of how or what percentage of the tithe each of these recipients ought to receive. Thus, each organization should receive the amount or percentage the giver wants to offer. However, there are ways to evaluate an organization and its management of money. We must remember that a tithing person's support for an organization ought constantly to come under review.

Which Recipient Should Receive More?

Which organizations should receive a greater percentage of the tithe, or gifts above the tithe standard? This can actually be a relatively simple matter. *The Christian steward must make his or her decision based upon the criterion of the recipient's money-management practices and the organization's effectiveness in doing God's work in the world.* For example, the giver can ask these simple questions in order to determine which recipient ought to receive more money.

1. Does the congregation, clergy discretionary fund, or relief organization to whom one gives have a stated mission and purpose for the use of offerings made to it? If not, why not? If so, then how effective is the organization or individual clergy person in the accomplishment of that stated goal. Churches and organizations that have no mission goals and that have no goals in general are usually ineffective in their allocation of funds. These organizations ought to receive less financial support until they have clear mission statements and until they develop stewardship and management practices to carry out those stated goals.

2. How much money is actually spent on the stated mission? Does a large portion go to overhead? Any organization which spends more than 75 percent of its income on overhead ought to be given less. The reason? Poor management and an inward-looking maintenance orientation is probably evident.

3. How open is the organization about its budget and spending practices? Are statements of its spending policies available to the public? If so, the organization deserves more money. If not, the organization ought to be watched closely for signs of mismanagement. To be sure, the organization ought to receive less until it is open and public about the way it spends donated funds.

Monitoring Recipients

Using these criteria to monitor organizations will help one to determine whether the recipients ought to receive a greater or lesser percentage of one's tithe. Monitoring also informs the organization of one's continuing interest and concern for its work. Any organization that does not want or appreciate a giver's constant attention and concern probably ought to be avoided until it is ready for such attention.

Debt

The average wage earner in the United States today has had no formal training in the management of household money, one's stipend. In America many of us are completely ignorant of the basic principles of good money management and investment practice. This is most evident in the alarming economic data available each year. Consumer debt in the United States is at historic levels. Americans spend more than any other people on earth and save very little of their income. Because of this, American families frequently find themselves in a bind during financial emergencies. When the crisis arises, the consumer heads to the bank for a loan. The result is more personal debt.

Any person who chooses to take up the philosophy of stewardship includes in their financial plan a response to this alarming trend. *For the Christian steward, debt is not a friend.* Debt is a destroyer of real wealth. For the purposes of discussion, debt may be defined as the mortgaging of the future in order to enable a purchase in the present. Unfortunately, the future is not always bright. Sometimes expenditures in the present are not payable in the future, and financial disaster follows. The Christian steward accepts the principle of living within one's means today. Living within one's means lessens, or even ends, debt; this increases the true wealth of the steward. The Christian steward is willing to sacrifice "having now" in order to "have more" later. The steward understands that the only way to accomplish the goal of having real secure wealth is to eradicate debt from his or her financial life. A well-planned budget will include a formula for the systematic elimination of debt.

Savings

A chief stumbling block to home ownership for many young American families today is not the scarcity of housing or mortgage money. Rather, a growing number of people are not disciplined enough to save the needed down payment. Unfortunately, while the cost of housing in the United States continues to rise, the savings rate for young Americans remains very low. Thus, home ownership is a financial problem for the young and, more than likely, a future problem for an aging American population. A budget in which Christian stewardship is practiced includes a plan to save enough for emergencies and for a down payment on a home. How? The Christian steward can begin by following these simple principles of saving.

Principles of Saving

First, *the Christian steward accepts the financial reality that mortgaging one's future in order to purchase consumable products now does not produce real wealth.* Real wealth is the accumulation of financial instruments or commodities that, over a period of time, appreciate in value. A home is a good example of one of the traditional ways to accumulate real wealth. By saving enough money for a down payment, a person may sacrifice the luxury of driving a new car every two or three years or travel less than he or she would like. But the willingness to sacrifice these things and not consume now can mean financial security in the future. The Christian steward recognizes that saving begins by accepting discipline. That discipline is simply a commitment to give up something now in order to get something in the future.

Second, *the Christian steward sets a primary financial goal of saving 10 percent of her or his gross income each month in an interest-bearing account.* This money is exclusively savings and for no other purpose. As we shall see, this goal may create some problems for budgeting, but the wealth-building benefits are so great that it is absolutely the quickest way to become financially secure.

Finally, *the Christian steward designs a budget that enables him or her to live on the remaining income.* This budget attempts to take into account all known expenses, and it provides for a contingency in emergencies. Thus, the steward follows the formula of giving 10 percent away, saving 10 percent for wealth building, and budgeting the remaining 80 percent for daily expenses.

Anyone who follows these principles will find their lives changed. But not in such a manner that they cannot continue to live with most of the same joy and happiness with which they lived before. The result, however, will be exciting: The Christian steward who follows these principles can succeed at saving and gain a deeper understanding of how personal discipline and sacrifice are truly worthwhile.

Everyday Expenses in the Budget

The bulk of the remaining 80 percent of one's income available after budgeting for sacrificial giving, debt relief, and savings is basically available for everyday expenses. The best way to budget this money is by categories of need. How much spending money does one want to carry around in one's pocket? How much do food and rent cost each month? What kind of clothing expenses are necessary during a month? What about fees and other little bits of income that we sometimes forget but that add up over the year? Of course, income taxes must be paid. Note, however, that for many taxpayers the contributions made to charity remain one of the best tax reduction factors. Since this is the case, some single and married people who tithe may find that their income taxes are somewhat lowered.

Most people know the real difficulty of living on a budget comes in the day-to-day discipline and grind of trying to stay within the planned expenses. The single biggest complaint of most people on a budget is that it is boring. This complaint is a real one. In fact, there is nothing exciting about staying on a budget. A budget is boring because in many cases the budget actually does anticipate all of one's needs. Since all of one's needs are accounted for, life seems safe and dull.

However, the Christian steward has a secret weapon in this battle of boredom. It is the regular joy produced by giving to and receiving from others and the joy of living for God's work beyond oneself. In addition, the Christian steward can see on a daily basis that this discipline is producing important results for the future.

Retirement Planning

Numerous elderly citizens of the United States retire each year. Unfortunately, many of them retire into poverty because years ago, in the post-World War II economic boom, they never bothered to develop a plan for retirement. Granted, a person is not always able to foresee all circumstances and plan for every economic turn of events. But the sad truth of the matter is that another generation of Americans appears to be repeating history. Young Americans appear almost unaware of the issue of retirement. Apparently, the majority are avoiding the simple action of making a plan for their exit from the work force in the next century. If this is true, economic disaster lies around the corner for many of them.

A person who makes a personal budget based upon a life of Christian stewardship includes a retirement plan A good retirement plan recognizes that planning must start early and that real accumulated wealth endures through almost any economic cycle or condition.

The Christian steward ought to ask whether an investment will have low risk and high value on a long-term basis. Diversify investments in order to take advantage of changing economic conditions. And finally, seek out the advice of reputable investment counselors who have expertise to judge the financial trends and requirements of a sound retirement portfolio.

Death and Taxes

Recent studies of the American Bar Association have shown that 60 percent of Americans who die each year do not have a will or a proper estate plan. The sad result is that their heirs must pay expensive fees in probate court. A probate court generally has one function. It decides how the estate will be divided among the heirs. One's survivors, especially if closely related, will receive some part of those worldly goods. However, in most states the costs for this are incredibly high. One's estate must pay the court costs and attorney's fees and, usually, numerous state and federal inheritance taxes. The heirs receive a very small portion of what one could have left them through a properly prepared will.

Unfortunately, the fact that fewer people have estate plans and wills leads to more and more court battles. Survivors want the estate preserved or passed on to heirs in a certain way, so they contest probate settlements. The result is even greater litigation cost to the heirs and to the estate.

A Christian steward accepts the reality of death and welcomes the opportunity to plan for the proper and just disposition of his or her worldly goods. The steward also includes in his or her estate plan a way to provide for God's work in the world even after death. This type of financial planning is called *planned giving*, and it is one of the most effective ways to control estate taxes. How?

The federal tax code (and those of many states as well) provides ways to exclude a person's estate from taxes through the creation of trusts. The Christian steward takes advantage of these laws by providing for a charitable gift to the church or to the work of God. At the same time, one shelters one's estate from unnecessary taxes. Best of all, this kind of estate planning can sometimes allow one's heirs to receive the full bulk of the estate without paying any tax. Believe it or not, this is all perfectly legal, so long as one has a properly prepared will. All that is necessary is to take time for proper planning and to hire a good tax attorney or accountant who wants to help the Christian steward plan for death.

A Sample Budget

Let us now look at what our outline of a Christian steward's budget might look like in a test case. Our example is the financial situation of an imaginary couple, John and Anne Ross. John is an engineer at a local aerospace firm in West Palm Beach, Florida. Anne just started teaching in a private school near their new home. This imaginary couple is typical of many Americans. First, let us consider John and Anne's situation before stewardship teaching becomes an important part of their financial lives and their faith.

John and Anne just purchased a new home for $138,900. Even though they have a relatively high joint income, they waited a long time to purchase their first home. They have not been able to buy a home before this year because they did not have enough savings for a down payment.

In the last seven years, John and Anne have been doing other things instead of saving. They have traveled extensively. John drives a new BMW, and Anne drives a Lincoln Mark VIII that is less than two years old. John and Anne do not have a budget to which they adhere. They presently have $7,500 in a money market account. Let us now look at a summary of John and Anne's income and expenses after ten years of marriage.

John and Anne Ross, West Palm Beach, Florida
John and Anne's Income

John's annual income for 1995 after 401k contributions	56,280.00
Anne's income	14,320.80
John and Anne's tax refund for 1994	1,023.20
Interest income	538.00
Total income	72,162.00

John and Anne's Expenses

Taxes	26,093.46
Mortgage and house expenses	18,000.00
Vacation and travel	10,389.00
Car payments	11,340.00
Food, clothing, personal needs	3,958.00
Other expenses	2,000.00
Contributions	381.54
Savings	.00
Total Expenses	72,162.00

John and Anne's Net Worth

Assets

House	138,900.00
BMW	23,800.00
Mark VIII	17,000.00
Savings	7,500.00
John's retirement	38,000.00
Other personal property	8,000.00
Total Assets	233,200.00

Liabilities

House mortgage	124,900.00
BMW loan payoff	24,300.00
Mark VIII loan payoff	18,200.00
Credit card debt	7,370.00
John's college loan	6,290.00
Other liabilities	754.00
Total liabilities	181,814.00
John and Anne's Net Worth	51,386.00

Discussion

At first glance, it seems that John and Anne have a wonderful life. They have visited a lot of wonderful places. They each drive new, stylish automobiles. They have recently purchased a new home, and still have a net worth of over fifty thousand dollars. This perception, however glamorous it may appear, is not quite accurate.

First, John is in his early forties. Anne is in her late thirties. For their ages, level of income, and their tax bracket (33 percent), they should have been in a position to purchase a home years ago. They have not taken advantage of important tax breaks they could have enjoyed long ago as home owners. These tax breaks would have helped increase John and Anne's net worth over the past ten years.

John's main asset is his 401k retirement fund at his place of employment. John had no choice about making contributions to this fund. These personal mandatory contributions have all been matched by John's company. He will not receive this money until he retires, over twenty years from now. So while John's retirement is well on the way to financial safety, his effective net worth is now actually $13,386.00. Part of his net worth is in personal property John owns, which might be very hard to sell if he needs cash.

John is still paying off a very large college loan even though he graduated long ago. The reason for this is that John has refinanced this loan at least twice over the past fifteen years. If he had not refinanced, the loan would have been paid off long ago. The interest rate for this loan is now very high. Refinancing the loan forced John to give up his special government-insured rate of 7 percent. He must now pay 14 percent.

In addition, John and Anne have very poor protection from a major health catastrophe. Although John has life and health insurance from his company, he has chosen benefits which carry high deductibles. These policies do not cover major medical problems. Some years ago John decided to choose these policy provisions because he and Anne were young. He also wanted to be paid the higher salary which the company offered to those who selected the higher deductible insurance policy. John's savings are not adequate now to cover a disability or a long-term illness.

Most of John and Anne's money has been spent on consumable items. The credit card expenses and the extensive vacations are connected. John has budgeted their vacations, but while traveling he and Anne have made additional purchases on their credit cards.

They now pay a minimum monthly bill to two banks for these debts.

Thus, John and Anne are hardly safe from any "wolf at the door." Their lavish living is evidence of their belief that they are safe from any problem. Unfortunately, this is a very risky way to live. It invites much pain and difficulty if some problem or health catastrophe occurs. John and Anne seem unaware that their lives are on an economic edge. Suddenly, something happens to start both Anne and John thinking.

John and Anne Have a Baby

Some time later, Anne begins to consider attending a stewardship seminar offered by their parish. Why? Although John has not been particularly active in their parish, Anne asks him to attend this seminar with her because she has suddenly become aware that her biological clock is running. Anne wants to have a baby.

After much discussion, John decides that he wants to have a child, too. Both John and Anne realize that this means their lifestyle will change drastically. So John agrees that the stewardship planning seminar is probably a good idea. Anne is happy John wants to go to this special event at their parish.

Anne thinks that both of them will have to make financial changes in their lives if they are to add another person to their family. Anne wonders if they spend too much money and live in too risky a financial lifestyle.

John and Anne are surprised to find on arriving that the leader of the workshop is a woman who is a professional certified financial planner hired to consult with the diocese. Her sole purpose in the seminar today is to teach parishioners more about good financial planning and to encourage parishioners to practice sound stewardship in their lives.

During the seminar, John and Anne are absolutely astounded by what they hear and see. First, John cannot imagine why anyone would consider giving large amounts of money to the church, or to any charity for that matter. Anne is shocked that, although they make over seventy thousand dollars a year, they cannot afford to have a child and maintain their present lifestyle.

The leader of the stewardship seminar notices that John and Anne are wide-eyed. She offers to speak with them afterward to work through some of their concerns. The stewardship leader first offers to formulate a new budget for John and Anne based upon sound stewardship practice. They accept her offer of help and wait while she formulates a proposed budget for them on her computer. When the computer printout is completed, the leader presents it to the couple. The computer printout looks like this:

John and Anne's Stewardship Budget

Total income	72,162.00

Proposed expenses for 1996

Taxes	24,543.00
Mortgage, etc.	18,000.00
Contributions	7,216.20
Savings	7,216.20
Car payments	5,100.00
Food, clothing	3,958.00
Other expenses (child care)	1,500.00
Baby sitters	1,200.00
Vacations	1,500.00
Credit card payments	1,000.00
Total expenses	71,233.40
Discretionary reserve	928.60

The stewardship leader explains to John and Anne that this budget enables them to give away at least 10 percent of their income and to save 10 percent for their future needs. In addition, the budget permits the annual development of a reserve fund for emergencies or unforeseen expenses.

John is impressed, but in looking over the budget, he notices that car expenses are dramatically lower. He also sees that first-class vacations are a thing of the past.

The stewardship leader breaks the bad news to John. Since his BMW is the only asset worth more than its loan payoff value, it is the best to liquidate. Thus, it must be sold to reduce expenses.

John objects. How would he get to work? The stewardship leader offers a simple solution. With the BMW sold, and the debt to the bank paid, John could use five thousand dollars from his money market fund to buy a small, late-model car. By paying cash for a used car, John would eliminate debt and lower expenses at the same time. In addition, the operating cost would be lower. This lower auto cost permits some additional money to be budgeted for credit card debt payoff. Now John and Anne can pay more than the minimum payment on each card. This will allow them to escape debt faster and save them even more money over the months ahead.

John objects again by asking why Anne should not sell her auto and drive a car more suitable for a young mother. In response to John, the stewardship leader points out that since Anne's auto is worth less now than the amount owed to the bank, Anne should continue to drive her Mark VIII. In a few years, this car's value will catch up with the amount owed. However, as soon as this happens, Anne also should consider selling her auto and purchasing a smaller car.

With tears in his eyes, John reluctantly agrees to sell the BMW.

As for the vacations, the stewardship leader reminds both John and Anne that an infant at home probably will make travel difficult for the next several years. The money budgeted for vacations could, therefore, be budgeted annually but saved until such time as they might take a first-class vacation with their child. John and Anne both think this a good idea.

Anne wonders out loud whether it would be possible for her to stay home after the baby is born. The stewardship leader explains that this is not an option. Because of their previous spending habits, Anne will have to continue to work for a while. The stewardship leader, however, points out to Anne that her school provides a free day-care service for its teachers. Anne can therefore work and visit the baby regularly during her breaks.

John again objects to giving so much money away. Why should he and Anne give so much to the church? John has never been that active and acknowledges that he does not even know the name of their priest. The stewardship leader listens to John's objections quietly. She then asks him a question. "John," she says, "What is the most important thing in your life?"

John is confused by this question. He asks what the stewardship leader means by it.

The stewardship leader responds, "Look at the expense report you made up for me in the workshop. Where are you spending the vast majority of your money right now?"

John looks at the report quietly. There are some moments of tense silence. Finally, he replies, "On ourselves. And then, I guess, on the government. "

The stewardship leader agrees. Then she asks, "What do you think this means for you, Anne, and the child you hope to have? What will your son or daughter learn from the way you spend your money?"

John is quiet for a long time. Finally, he replies, "He or she will learn that taking care of number one comes first. But that's the way the world is."

"Yes," says the stewardship leader, "It is the way the world is. But do you want your child to learn only the way of the world? What about learning that a person can take care of their own needs but be generous toward the church and make the church an important part of your life financially. If you teach your child why you are generous, your child will see that God and the church are both important to you. Your child will also see that it is possible to be a generous person and still look out for one's own interests. Think about that."

John and Anne thank the stewardship leader for her time. The stewardship leader encourages both John and Anne to accept the budget and begin their journey of giving. She also encourages them to go to an attorney and have wills drawn for themselves.

John and Anne leave the church in silence. In the next few weeks, they discuss the workshop, the proposed budget, the baby, and the tithe to the church. They go to an attorney and have proper wills drawn. But John and Anne continue to struggle with what they might do.

What We Can Learn from John and Anne

The case of John and Anne is a common one. They want to change their lives in order to include a new member in the family. This causes them both to think seriously about their future and their financial lives together.

The financial plan that the stewardship leader offers to John and Anne is sound. It shifts their lifestyle away from consuming and debt and toward a future of building wealth. This radical financial change begins the process of eliminating debt and other liabilities. In addition, the budget guards against problems resulting from a major illness because it emphasizes the importance of savings and planning for unforeseen events.

By making wills for themselves, John and Anne have eliminated another problem that could occur should they die accidentally. Their heir will receive their estates exclusive of any other relatives. This means their child will have a means of support. The will also provides for legal guardians to be appointed and trusts to come into force.

Many good things come out of their experience in the stewardship workshop. Nevertheless, it presents John, in particular, with a stumbling block. He has a real problem with the idea of giving money "away" to the church. Until John and Anne resolve this issue, they probably will not decide to live on the budget the stewardship leader has prepared for them.

At the foundation of this struggle for John is a spiritual issue of the power of money. John has not been active in the church. He does not really want to face the decision the stewardship leader places before him. Should he make the church a primary organization into which he invests his life and his money, or should he try to live on the budget without the financial commitment to tithe? It would be an act of faith for John to tithe to the church. This is especially the case because John doesn't see in his own values and lifestyle a real need to do so.

John and Anne must together decide between a life of stewardship and a life without theological groundings. If they decide to take the risk of the tithe and the budget, they will ultimately experience a new dimension of life. Their lives will be changed forever, both economically and spirituality. For if John and Anne decide to give up control over their money and give it away, they will have acted in faith and be living in a new covenant in which risk is real.

What will John and Anne decide to do? This cannot be predicted. It will come down to how they work through the issues and how they make their decision. The matter will probably be decided through the process of struggle. John does not know it, but he will struggle with the values of what it means to be in covenant with God in Christ and the values and priority of money. John and Anne hold dear many values about money. Thus, their struggle is the universal struggle all Christians face in relation to stewardship. We will wait to hear what decision they make for themselves.

Tithing Begins with a Crucial Decision

Obviously, the tithe is a symbol of a person's spiritual and financial commitment. In a practical sense, this commitment is decided every day in the way each of us spends our money. Do we first give to others, to God's work, and to the work of the church and then take care of our own budgetary needs? Or do we spend first on ourselves, and then give whatever is left to God's work?

Also, do we tithe and budget in such a way that we reduce the stress of debt and economic peril hanging over our heads? Or do we continue to live in a kind of self-induced slavery to money? The message of Jesus Christ is that God wants all of us to be free from the power of economic pressure and to live happy lives of management through which we strive to be the best people we can be. This, however, can only happen when we are willing to take a risk to discipline ourselves economically and tithe sacrificially to God's work.

In our next chapter, we shall examine this struggle from a different viewpoint, that of covenant theology. We shall also complete our study by examining the remaining question: What is a tithe?

CHAPTER SIX

The Practice of the Tithe, Covenant Theology, and the Pilgrimage of Giving

A person who chooses to enter into a covenant vortex with Jesus Christ at his or her baptism does so on many levels of interrelationship.

In the last chapter, John and Anne Ross were offered as examples of a typical American household. Both of them were challenged, because of a change in their plans for the future, to modify their way of living. Although John and Anne had not been very active Christians in their local parish, in their time of need they sought out their church's help. This tendency to seek out the church in a time of transition is not uncommon. Many inactive Christians turn to the church when they feel they need help with a life issue.

In attending the stewardship seminar, John and Anne demonstrated a willingness to consider alternative financial plans and to modify their lifestyle. As the seminar concluded, John was particularly troubled. More than anything, the emphasis on the tithe troubled him.

The stewardship leader recognized that John was struggling with tithing. Although not a clergy person, she responded to John and Anne in a pastoral manner. She offered to provide them with some of her professional time, free of charge. She went to great lengths to make John feel comfortable with her. Even though she differed from him in her views, she remained quiet and calm as John offered reasons for his objections to tithing. The stewardship leader attempted to respond to John's concerns by offering a long-term and family-oriented description of what giving sacrificially can mean for a person and a family.

John did not accept the stewardship leader's explanation. In fact, John made it clear that his values were quite different from hers.

The irony of this encounter, however, is that while John did not, in fact, accept the stewardship leader's advice with regard to the tithe, John did trust her to give him financial advice and counsel. For example, John trusted her enough to accept the advice to sell his car but not enough to change his giving behavior and accept the tithe as his standard of giving. Unfortunately, he could not envision for himself the deeper spiritual issues, which the stewardship leader was attempting to help him grasp. John simply did not understand that money frequently exerts an adverse influence on a person's life, especially if money becomes the center of that life. The stewardship leader tried to help John understand that no one can be free from enslavement to money until he or she makes a commitment to enter into God's covenant through sacrificial giving.

We have seen in chapter 5 that the tithe must enjoy the first position in a well-planned stewardship budget. Now we shall devote ourselves to the remaining practical issue of how one goes about the process of tithing. How does one calculate a tithe? How does one start to tithe? What is the theological meaning of the tithe for a person who is willing to give it a try? We shall attempt to answer these questions in a systematic fashion.

How Does One Calculate a Tithe?

As already noted above, in the ancient tradition of Israel, the tithe is frequently discussed but rarely defined for daily practice. Moreover, we have seen that when calculation of the tithe is mentioned in Hebrew Scripture, it is usually connected with the doctrine of the first fruits of all land and produce. In the modern world, where commissions, salaries, 401k pension plans, and annuities are part of a general worker's compensation package, the comparison of the first fruits tradition to modern tithe calculation is practically impossible, except perhaps for the farmer.

In other words, for the modern worker, the calculation of a tithe according to biblical terms and traditions is filled with problems and possible exceptions. For the purpose of this discussion we will not attempt to account for all the problems and exceptions but will offer guidelines for the modern Christian's calculation of a tithe. These guidelines are not perfect but will provide some clarity and highlight advantages for taking up the practice of tithing.

Guidelines for Calculation of a Tithe

As we have noted in our study of the Hebrew Scriptures, the calculated amount of money in a tithe can best be determined, and is most faithful to the Hebrew tithing tradition, when it is based upon *annual gross income.*

It must be remembered that ancient Israel had no such thing as an income tax in the modern sense. Thus, the notion of paying taxes to the state, and then paying a tithe to the Temple, was almost completely foreign to Judaism. For the religious Hebrew, the tithe was an extension of the covenant relationship. Thus, the amount of the tithe appears to have been calculated upon the annual gross harvest of an Israelite's farm, or upon an Israelite's annual gross income from work. Theologically, in most cases, the tithe was not considered to be a tax or understood as such. But as we have seen, the tithe is in a few cases discussed in Hebrew Scripture as a kind of levied tax. So it is difficult to address this issue with clarity.

In modern America, an additional problem arises: establishing one's annual gross income for the calculation of a tithe.

There exist many different ways today to determine a person's annual gross income. Some people calculate their gross income based upon their total commissions and/or salaries for the year. Others first exclude money placed into pension plans, annuities and other tax-free instruments. Then they calculate their gross income on the remaining amount.

Moreover, other kinds of financial instruments are commonly part of a compensation package. These instruments can actually change the way gross income is calculated. For example, the simple act of opening an IRA account can make the determination of a person's annual gross income much more complicated and controversial.

For the purposes of this study, it is possible to offer a solution for the problems of defining gross income by establishing the following guideline: *Annual gross income includes all income listed and totaled on page 1 of a person's annual United States Internal Revenue Service tax return.*

For example, John and Anne Ross's gross income for 1995 is listed on the front page of their 1040 tax return as $72,162.00. Thus, a tithe for John and Anne can be calculated as $7,216.20, or 10 percent of their gross income figure for the calendar year. The question immediately arises, however, what about all of John's perks? For example, John's annual gross income on his tax return does not reflect the tax-free payments he made to his company retirement plan. Shouldn't these payments be included in the tithe calculation?

It is true that John was compelled by company policy to contribute a significant amount of his income to his retirement plan. But, for all intents and purposes, John will neither spend nor pay taxes on that money until he is retired. For this reason, the federal government does not consider the money paid to the retirement fund taxable income for 1995. However, when John begins drawing income from his retirement plan, he will at that time pay taxes on money he withdraws from the fund each year.

Now if John were a tithing person and he decided to include the money he placed in his retirement fund as part of his gross income figure, he would certainly be doing a noble thing. But it would create a problem. John's future calculation of the tithe during his retirement years would suddenly become far more difficult. How? Well, to be fair, the present annual contribution to the church should be taken into consideration during his retirement. And calculating an annual tithe of his retirement income after many years of tax-free interest accrual would be difficult.

Obviously, for John, the simplest way to calculate a tithe is to determine the amount based on his annual gross federal taxable income. Years from now, when John retires and he begins to receive money from his company retirement fund, he and Anne may decide to tithe. It would then be appropriate for John to tithe his annual income from his retirement fund, too.

How Often Does One Pay a Tithe?

Once the annual income for the year is properly calculated, it becomes possible to tithe to the parish annual budget, to the clergy discretionary fund, or to any other fund that qualifies under the guidelines set forth above. However, what is the best way to pay this money? Does one pay the money in one lump sum, monthly, or otherwise? What is the best form of payment for the recipient and the tithing person?

The most highly recommended guideline is to *give on a weekly basis to one's local parish.* Other offerings can be made *on an occasional basis.* Regular weekly offerings to the parish are preferred for several important reasons.

First, weekly offerings enable the parish to function on a financially steady and reliable income. Cash flow problems for congregations are significantly lessened when the majority of members are willing to make their payments in regular weekly installments.

Second, regular weekly offerings provide an increased opportunity for spiritual growth. By paying one's tithe on a weekly basis, the Christian disciple gains an enriched experience of life as a Christian steward. Each weekly payment reminds the steward of the meaning of sacrifice. Giving money weekly allows the steward to grasp the spiritual importance of the freedom to give.

Finally, weekly offering to the parish encourages the steward to attend services regularly. After all, if a steward is not there to make his or her financial offering, it becomes more difficult to keep up regular weekly giving. Also, the regular gift each week forces a steward to stay on budget and to monitor spending activity with integrity. This is an important element in the development of financial discipline, and it becomes a spot check that helps one stay within the defined limits of the budget.

How Does One Begin Tithing?

Taking up the tithe as a weekly form of giving is not easy for many Christians. These people inevitably ask whether there is a less painful way to begin to tithe, rather than to give systematically 10 percent of their income. We will offer a few guidelines to make the transition less of a struggle, and the practice of tithing more psychologically and emotionally acceptable.

The best method for beginning the pilgrimage of giving and making the tithe more acceptable is called *progressive percentage giving.* Progressive percentage giving begins with a stated percentage of one's annual income and then progressively increases the percentage until one reaches 10 percent—or an amount beyond—within a projected length of time.

For example, if John and Anne Ross were to decide to tithe, they might begin by making an offering of 5 percent of their income to their parish. John and Anne would then offer a higher percentage each of the next two years until they were tithing. Thus, they could be tithing within a three-year period.

Progressive percentage giving is an excellent way to begin the pilgrimage of sacrificial giving. In the case of John, progressive percentage giving might also have another distinct advantage. Over the three-year period, John might be able to work through some of his personal problems about tithing and sacrificial giving. Progressive percentage giving is especially helpful for those who have reservations about the practice of tithing.

How Is One's Spiritual Growth Linked to Tithing?

Now we must address the question of how the tithe is related to the journey of faith, which has been mentioned so often in this study. As we have seen, all offerings of oneself to God originate from a devout desire to glorify and to thank God for the fulfillment of promises made in a covenant. Thankfulness and praise are the natural result of an awareness of God's faithfulness and God's gift of salvation. For the Christian, the gift of salvation is understood primarily in the sacrifice of the life and death and rising of Jesus Christ. Through Christ, a new covenant has been bestowed on those who will receive it. In this covenant, God promises salvation to those who believe in God's Son and who are willing to serve and to work for the fulfillment of God's kingdom on earth.

We have also seen that this Christian covenant has its initial foundation in each Christian through the sacrament of Baptism. When one is baptized, one is bound to Jesus Christ in the covenant of redemption and kingdom discipleship. In the world, the primary work of a disciple is to be a steward of God's message of salvation and to offer God the gifts one has to offer. In other words, stewardship is the main work of all church members and of any person bound to Jesus Christ in covenant.

The nature of entrance into the covenant of Jesus Christ enables a disciple to begin a pilgrimage of faith. For the Christian steward, as we have seen in Jesus' parables, faith is turning over control of one's will and one's personal history to God. Faith is a willingness to include God in one's personal history and to take up God's agenda in the world.

At the foundation of life in the covenant is spiritual growth, which is part of the pilgrimage of giving. As we have seen in our examination of his letters, Paul makes it very clear that, by pouring out ourselves for God's sake, we become filled with God's Spirit. Anyone bound in covenant with Jesus Christ can find the economy of salvation in daily living in the divine covenant.

The Nature of Covenant

Throughout this entire study, we have seen that all giving, both in Christianity and in Judaism, emanates from covenant life. Throughout our study, we have offered the covenant concept as the guiding force for stewardship and true spiritual giving. Now we must define what we mean by covenant in the Christian sense of everyday existence in the divine economy of God. This is a difficult task.

For the modern person, the notion of covenant is almost unknown or at least unrecognizable. Like any relationship, however, the covenant with Jesus Christ is real. It is a relationship with boundaries and describable characteristics. Let us now examine these important elements.

Christian Covenant

A Christian can recognize that he or she is in a covenant with Jesus Christ when daily life with God encompasses a changing relationship between spiritual polarities *represented by the center and edges of a vortex.* A vortex is defined in *Webster's New World Dictionary* as "any activity, situation, or state of affairs that resembles a whirl or eddy in its rush, absorbing affect, catastrophic power, etc." Life with Jesus Christ is like a vortex. As a person participates in the covenant, one is drawn toward the gift of God's grace and ultimate salvation. Life in the covenant is a life in the world, but that world is also in the vortex with God.

A person who chooses to enter into a covenant vortex with Jesus Christ at his or her baptism does so on many levels. A model of this vortex relationship contains a polarity. That is, a Christian lives in a tension between what one presently and authentically is as a person in the world and what one can be in the future—between the edges and the center.

These elements of relationship emanate out of human existence and, in particular, out of ancient Israel's experience of existence in covenant with God. However, many of the characteristics of covenant life are just as prominent today in the Christian experience with Jesus Christ. For the Christian, the elements of covenant life with Jesus Christ in the vortex are many. But for the purpose of discussion I have limited the elements here to seven. We now turn to a description of each of the seven elements of polarity in the Christian covenant.

Risk versus Safety

A person who enters a covenant vortex with Jesus Christ constantly deals with the question of whether the relationship is safe or risky. The nature of Christian faith, as we have already seen in the study of Jesus' parables, is willingly to take a risk in one's life, to lose control of one's history by giving it to God. Sometimes one feels more willing to take a risk than at other times. We have seen that the people of Israel were called into a covenant with God in which risk played a major role. In the Hebrew Scriptures, the risk of being drawn into the vortex of covenant salvation always appears to frighten the people of Israel.

In our example, John was not willing to enter into the covenant through systematic giving. Although John was willing to risk embarrassment with his friends and others by taking the advice of the workshop leader to sell his BMW, he was not willing to risk entering into what appeared to be a very unclear relationship with the church or the Divine. For John, God seemed irrelevant to the issue of financial planning. He could not see that his inability to save money and his free-spending habits of the past revealed his true values.

By asking John to tithe, the stewardship leader offered him the opportunity to enter into the vortex of Christian covenant. John, however, saw that this offer of life in the vortex placed his whole value system at risk. The offer of covenant did, in fact, bring John into a state of reflection, but he chose safety. He felt safer on the edge than plunging into the whirl of the vortex.

Risk versus safety can be a fundamental factor in many human relationships. But in a faith relationship with God, the willingness to risk is foundational. John took no chances at all and, therefore, failed to enter into the vortex of covenant.

Response versus Ambivalence

The second element of the covenant vortex is that of response versus ambivalence. In this dynamic, life in the covenant depends on caring. How much does one care to respond to one's life and history? If a person cares, he or she will respond. Ambivalence is the lack of response or caring. It means floating through life without commitment, circling on the edge of the spinning vortex.

We have seen that in the case of his parables, Jesus of Nazareth called Israel out of its ambivalence and into responsiveness to the covenant. But the leaders of Israel responded with ambivalence.

For John Ross, the element of response versus ambivalence was, in fact, a crucial aspect of his encounter with the stewardship leader. The stewardship leader invited John to enter into the vortex of a covenant relationship with God. This moment of invitation was most clear when she told him that his willingness to give to the church would have long-lasting implications for his family's understanding of responsibility for self and for others. Unfortunately, John demonstrated a degree of ambivalence about the value of this. John's attitude revealed that, while he was deeply concerned that his family have a good example of responsibility, he did not see how tithing might relate to the issue. The paradox was that though John was, in fact, a generally responsible person in his daily work and in his family life, in terms of being drawn into covenant with God, he was also ambivalent. In many ways, John's ambivalence held him back from giving the tithe and the covenant a try.

Trust versus Mistrust

The third element of the covenant vortex is that of trust versus mistrust. This dynamic will be familiar to readers of the psychological investigations of Eric Erikson. In the dynamic of trust versus mistrust, a person seeking to live in covenant with God is always attempting to learn new ways how to make a trusting bond with God and with others. In interpersonal relationships, the need for trust is primary. Such is also the case for anyone in a covenant relationship with God. Trust or mistrust is always a fundamental underlying concern.

As we have seen in the parables of Jesus, covenant life includes the daily struggle to trust God's promises today and in the near future.

John, while a believer in God and a baptized person, was not willing to enter into a vortex in which he would be drawn into trust with God. John's need for safety was so great that he could not allow himself to enter into a covenant relationship in which he might discover that he could trust the power of God more than he trusted the power of his money. John chose to remain on the edge of the vortex of the covenant.

Management versus Manipulation

The fourth element of the covenant vortex is management versus manipulation. Management is the appropriate use of power and skill to gain a just, equitable, and efficient living. On the other hand, manipulation is the unjust use of power or skill to create personal opportunity. It is the selfish use of power to enhance one's position or one's livelihood.

As we have seen in our examination of Jesus' parables, management is a fundamental teaching of Jesus. Life in the covenant with God means a person repeatedly struggles to move from manipulation to management.

All of us are prone to manipulate others. However, not all of us are capable managers of people or resources. In a relationship with God, we can become more willing to recognize and struggle with our tendency to manipulate. We can also get in touch with our tendency to exploit others. After this reflective recognition begins, the character of covenant life draws us to move away from manipulation toward the goal of learning new, ethical management skills.

John felt that the stewardship leader was attempting to manipulate him into giving money to the church. It did not occur to John that the fundamental issue at stake for him and Anne might be the appropriate and just management of their money. The stewardship leader's advice to tithe countered John's own values. Thus, her suggestions appeared to him to be manipulation. He did not see how this woman, a consultant for the diocese, might have the right to advise him about giving away his money. He failed to recognize that the stewardship leader in no way pressured him and would not have gained any personal reward from John's tithe.

If John took a risk and allowed himself to be drawn into a covenant relationship with Christ, he might become open to self-examination. This might reveal to him that he sometimes tries to manipulate others—and even God. Unfortunately, John is not open to personal evaluation of his motives. He resists being drawn into the vortex of covenant with God.

Inspiration versus Obligation

The fifth element of covenant in the vortex is that of inspiration versus obligation. As we have seen in our study of covenant in the Hebrew Scriptures, ancient Israel was always struggling with life between these two poles. Sometimes Hebrew writers argued for the spirit of life in the covenant. Other times they appealed to simple obligation.

The Spirit is a gift God bestows on people drawn into Christian covenant. As this process of receiving spiritual gifts takes place in a person, each individual becomes more free to give to and receive from others—and from God—without a sense of obligation.

For John Ross, inspiration seemed a distant issue unrelated to his goal of developing a financial plan. It did not occur to him that there might be a spiritual benefit for him and for his family in a commitment of his money to God's work through the church.

This point did not occur to John because he was not really interested in receiving anything from God. John was actually interested in attaining his goal of developing a new financial plan for his family. He did not expect to receive anything as a result of tithing. Giving up control of some money seemed only to promise a tighter budget. In the end, he was not drawn into covenant with God because of his sense of financial obligation.

Love versus Fear

The sixth element of covenant life in the vortex is the struggle between love for versus fear of God. Living in the covenant vortex means to develop such a sense of familiarity with God that one no longer fears but loves God. When drawn into the vortex of covenant, we let go of our fear and learn a new way of relating to God and to others. That way of relating is grounded in love.

As we have seen in the Hebrew Scriptures, fear is a common Hebrew covenant issue. Fear that Yahweh would not fulfill the promises to Israel was a common element in the Hebrew tradition. But also in the tradition of Israel, love for God was hailed as the pinnacle of faith in the covenant. Israel was always struggling between these two poles of existence.

Our study of the parables of Jesus has revealed a similar dynamic of love for Yahweh versus fear of Yahweh's coming judgment. Jesus constantly calls Israel to faith and into a deepening love for Yahweh through images of paradox. In God's coming reign, God's love will be valuable beyond anything in this life, more valuable than fine pearls or hidden treasure.

John Ross neither loves nor fears God. Thus, he sees God and his relationship with God as a peripheral matter. John Ross is still out on the edge of the vortex.

In a covenant with God, however, the key to spiritual growth is investing oneself in God's kingship through love, as opposed to acting on behalf of God because of fear. For example, a person can go to church services every Sunday and yet be lacking in spiritual growth. This can happen when a person's motivation for church attendance is grounded in a fear of condemnation by God. Someone who attends church for this reason is certainly not in a mode conducive to receiving grace from God. Real growth in grace occurs when a person is willing to be drawn into the vortex and receive from God what God has to offer: love. In order to do this, a person must grow secure enough in love for God to overcome their fear of judgment and of the future unknown.

Justice versus Injustice

The seventh and final polar element in the covenant vortex is justice versus injustice. Justice is action in life that produces equality and dignity for all people. Injustice is the treatment of others that causes inequality and a loss of dignity.

People drawn into a covenant with God through Jesus Christ most certainly struggle with this polarity. One finds oneself constantly struggling to determine whether actions taken in the world are just or unjust. It takes a growth in courage and sometimes a willingness to oppose the majority to become a just person.

In the case of ancient Israel, justice versus injustice was a continuing issue in the Hebrew covenant. In Hebrew Scripture, Israel might in one moment be just and in the next, unjust. It all depended on Israel's willingness to seek Yahweh's divine will.

In John Ross's situation, it was John's view that justice had nothing to do with the creation of his financial plan. In fact, his values and his ethics were based on looking out for his own needs. For example, John never previously questioned his financial lifestyle and the justice of it in relation to his wife, Anne. However, by telling John that she wanted to have a baby, Anne forced him to examine his conduct in light of this new situation. Quite possibly, therefore, John never would have changed his high-spending ways if not for the necessity to plan ahead.

John never thought it unjust that he controlled the money and spent it without creating savings for the future. There were even times when John spent money without discussing it with Anne. This was why Anne was uncomfortable with their lifestyle. When the family's situation changed with a coming child, Anne and the stewardship leader realized that John's financial philosophy was fundamentally unjust to her and to their child's future. John's habits and bad spending practices provided no money for the child or for the future security of the family. If John were to die or be disabled suddenly, the family would be in terrible financial difficulty. Thus, John's values and his lifestyle were fundamentally selfish and unjust.

In a Christian covenant with God, a person is always willing to reflect upon his or her actions in relation to the issue of justice. Sometimes this process is an emotional struggle, but it is also a necessary part of being in a redemptive relationship with God.

Life in the Covenant Vortex

A person who is drawn into a covenant with God through Jesus Christ begins the struggle with these polar aspects of life. Very often these distinct and important struggles occur simultaneously, and each is important. In one moment, a person can be dealing with the issues of risk versus safety, justice versus injustice, and love versus fear. Or all seven elements can come to bear upon an issue. Daily life in covenant with God is ever changing and requires new growth and personal development.

> *Salvation comes to a person who is willing to be drawn*
> *into and remain in the vortex of the covenant at all times.*

This is a fundamental principle. Since life in the covenant makes it possible for God to bestow salvation upon us, we must remain in the covenant at all times and forever. This is why our covenant vows made at baptism are considered by the church to be indissoluble. If we are to receive the gift of salvation from God, we must be willing to remain in the vortex of covenant life forever.

Life in the covenant vortex is not safe or comfortable; it is a struggle for spiritual and personal growth. So it is tempting for many Christians to try to avoid life in the covenant. They think this kind of life is too difficult and unpleasant an experience to sustain on a long-term basis. But for those who commit themselves to it, life in the vortex is not unpleasant at all! In fact, the struggle of growth actually feels good and the benefits are numerous.

> *In covenant life, there is no purely good nor*
> *purely evil person.*

None of the polar elements mentioned above makes a person either totally good or completely evil. No one breaks out of the polar tension and achieves all those things that are good. For example, no person in the covenant is just at all times. Yet it is tempting to believe that one's covenant journey towards becoming a just person leads to perfection. No Christian in covenant with Jesus Christ can ever attain perfect justice in this life. One must be satisfied with life as it is—a life in which one grows toward becoming a more just person.

If the salvation process were actually a demand of God for perfection—in risk, justice, spiritual growth, and all the other elements of the covenant vortex—human beings could save themselves by sheer will power. Rather, all of us must seek to become better people by joining with God in a special relationship in which giving and receiving are fundamental. In a life of being drawn into the vortex, perfection is a spiritual gift, a status bestowed by God through divine grace. This means that a person's authentic faith begins with an acceptance that he or she must live in a whirlwind relationship with God. Within the whirlwind, a voice calls each person toward perfection. For Christians, the voice in the whirlwind belongs to Jesus Christ.

The final key to covenant life has to do with tithing and stewardship.

> *The only continuous and constant way to stay in the*
> *covenant vortex for any long period of time is to be*
> *a sacrificial giver of one's time, talent and treasure*
> *to the glory of Jesus Christ and to the fulfillment*
> *of God's kingdom on earth.*

The offering of time, talent, and money to God enables one to lose sufficient control over one's life so that one is drawn into the covenant vortex. The tithe is one of the most sacrificial ways to offer one's money. To give beyond the tithe is to risk even more, increasing one's freedom from control and freedom to give. To give from one's financial resources beyond the tithe is to invest one's life in the covenant vortex in the most spectacular and impressive manner. This sacrifice provides the platform for the coming of the grace of God.

Christian Stewardship and the Tithe:
A Pilgrimage of Giving

The tithe is the spiritual and financial key for Christian life, and life in the vortex is a spiritual and financial pilgrimage. It is a spiritual pilgrimage toward oneness with God and a surrender of one's self to the divine will. One embarks on a pilgrimage of giving as a steward for whom new attitudes and a new lifestyle become possible.

Life in the covenant is a financial pilgrimage. By giving, each person begins to learn just how much power their money has over their lives. It can be a struggle because Christ calls into question much of what a person is upon entrance into covenant. Just as Jesus called Israel into question for its lack of faith in the covenant, so does he call us to reexamine our motives and our values.

Life in the Christian vortex is a pilgrimage. The basis of this pilgrimage is the challenge to grow in love and to give up fear as one's motivation in life. In this life risk becomes preferable to safety. We grow aware that Jesus Christ is our friend, not our enemy. In this covenant we realize that God wants to love and guide us into freedom and salvation.

The tithe is, therefore, a spiritual key for any Christian. It is a minimum standard of giving for anyone who wishes to abide in the covenant vortex and lose control of one's will for God. Through the tithe, God's future can be opened to a person. The tithe frees us to discover God and God's history for ourselves.

For the greater mission of the church, the tithe empowers the local congregation and other church agencies in the world, which represent the work of Jesus Christ, to reach out and do that work. The tithe can be the means by which those who give and those who receive enter into the covenant vortex with Jesus Christ.

So the great challenge for all Christians today is to give themselves away as a living sacrifice to God. The challenge is to permit ourselves to be drawn into the vortex, where Christ waits to direct and remake each one of us. We all have reason to share the covenant of Jesus Christ with the Church. All of us have reason to take up our pilgrimage. For in that relationship we all find salvation and our real personhood as people of God.

NOTES

Chapter One

1. Albert Schweitzer, *Out of My Life and Thought*, trans. C. T. Campion (New York: Holt, Rinehart and Winston, 1961), 23 *ff.*

Chapter Two

1. For an excellent introduction to the research of Hebrew Scripture, see: Georg Fohrer, *Introduction to the Old Testament*, trans. David L. Green (Nashville: Abingdon Press., 1966), 103-195.

2. *Jerusalem Bible*, ed. Alexander Jones (Garden City, NY: Doubleday, 1966). All subsequent biblical citations are taken from this translation unless otherwise noted.

3. A similar view of the tithe as a kind of tax is found in Jth. 11:13; Tob. 1:6-8; and Sir. 35: 8-9.

Chapter Three

1. See Helmut Koester, *Introduction to the New Testament* (Philadelphia: Fortress Press, 1982), 43-56.

2. For an excellent and complete history of research on the New Testament, see Werner Georg Kummel, *The New Testament: The History of the Investigation of Its Problems*, trans. S. Gilmour and Howard C. Kee (Nashville: Abingdon Press, 1972). Also see Patrick Henry, *New Directions in New Testament Study* (Philadelphia: Westminster Press, 1979).

3. See E. P. Sanders, *Jesus and Judaism* (Philadelphia: Fortress Press, 1985), 123-244.

4. Adolf Julicher, *Die Gleichnisreden Jesu* (1910; reprint, Darmstadt: Wissenschaftliche Buchgesellschaft, 1976).

5. Ibid, 259-585.

6. C. H. Dodd, *The Parables of the Kingdom*, rev. ed. (New York: Charles Scribner's Sons, 1961), 5.

7. Ibid, 13-19.

8. Ibid, 19*f.*

9. I have preferred the version of this parable found in Mark over that found in Luke13:18-19 or Matt.13:31*f.* C. H. Dodd and others have argued that this version in Mark is inferior to that found in Luke. However, there are sufficient reasons to doubt the value of the Lukan version over Mark. First, although the parable in Luke's version is apparently more simple than Mark in its style and language, we must assume editorial changes on the part of both Luke and Matthew, not of Mark. Second, the version of Mark is closer to a version of the same parable found in the sayings source called *The Gospel of Thomas* (saying 20). Many scholars consider Thomas to be older than Mark. Thus, the version in Mark is more appropriate for our study.

10. Dodd, *Parables*, 19.

11. A graph is simply a representation of the parable mapped out on paper. It is a way to detect patterns and structures in the parable story.

12. Contrast this fact with the versions of the parable in Matt.13:24-30 and Luke 13:18 where the human figure is present. This demonstrates well the tendency of both Matthew and Luke to allegorize the parable for their own purposes.

13. In the ancient world, it was common for farmers to believe that nothing could sprout until it first died as a seed. This theme of dying and coming back to life is frequently used in the New Testament.

14. In Matthew's Gospel, the phrase "kingdom of God" is slightly modified by Matthew to "kingdom of heaven." Most scholars believe that this small change to the tradition was made in order to avoid speaking or writing the sacred name for God, Yahweh. In Jewish circles, speaking or writing this word was considered a sin. Matthew has been highly influenced by this Jewish tradition.

15. See Joachim Jeremias, *The Parables of Jesus*, 2nd rev. ed. (New York: Charles Scribner's Sons, 1972), 90*f*. See also Bernard Brandon Scott, *Hear Then the Parable, A Commentary on the Parables of Jesus* (Fortress Press, Minneapolis, 1989). See also T. W. Manson, *The Sayings of Jesus* (London, 1950).

Chapter Four

1. References are found in Luke 11:42; 18:12; and Matt. 23:23-24.

2. A clear and excellent explanation of the relationships among the first three Gospels can be found in Howard Clark Kee, *Jesus in History*, 2nd ed. (New York: Harcourt Brace Jovanovich, 1977), 9-212. More recently, see Luke T. Johnson, *The Writings of the New Testament* (Philadelphia: Fortress Press, 1986), 144-240.

3. On the nature of Q, see the excellent summary in Kee, *Jesus in History*, 76-120.

4. See Eduard Schweizer, *The Good News According to Mark*, trans. Donald H. Madvig, (Atlanta: John Knox Press, 1970), 208-215.

5. Controversy continues over which of Paul's letters are genuine and which are edited or entirely composed by writers using the name of Paul. For an excellent introduction to the problem of authenticity, see Werner G. Kummel, *Introduction to the New Testament*, rev. ed., trans. Howard C. Kee (Nashville: Abingdon Press, 1987), 255-366.